The
Fruit, Herbs & Vegetables
of Italy

Lucy, Countess of Bedford. Circle of Robert Peake

GIACOMO CASTELVETRO

The Fruit,
Herbs & Vegetables
of Italy

AN
OFFERING TO
LUCY, COUNTESS OF BEDFORD

TRANSLATED WITH AN INTRODUCTION BY
Gillian Riley

FOREWORD BY
Jane Grigson

VIKING

BRITISH MUSEUM, NATURAL HISTORY

For

J.M.M.

Cascan le rose e restan poi le spine:
Non giudicate nulla innanzi il fine.

Viking

Published by the Penguin Group
27 Wrights Lane, London W8 5TZ, England
Viking Penguin Inc., 40 West 23rd Street, New York, New York 10010, USA
Penguin Books Australia Ltd, Ringwood, Victoria, Australia
Penguin Books Canada Ltd, 2801 John Street, Markham, Ontario, Canada L3R 1B4
Penguin Books (NZ) Ltd, 182–190 Wairau Road, Auckland 10, New Zealand

Penguin Books Ltd, Registered Offices: Harmondsworth, Middlesex, England

First published 1989
1 3 5 7 9 10 8 6 4 2

Introduction & Translation copyright © Gillian Riley, 1989

Foreword © Jane Grigson, 1989

Designed by Gillian Riley

Filmset in Galliard by Wyvern Typesetting Limited, Bristol

Printed in Great Britain by
William Clowes Ltd, Beccles and London

A CIP catalogue record for this book is available from the British Library

ISBN 0-670-82724-X

Contents

Angelica. Jacopo Ligozzi (1547–1627)

Foreword

Where I first read the name of Castelvetro, I cannot clearly recall. It seems to me that it was in the Linnaean Library, in 1976 or 1977. I was writing a book on vegetables at the time, and I had gone to the library to look at Parkinson's *Paradisi in Sole Paradisus Terrestris* and Thomas Martyn's 1807 edition of Philip Miller's *Gardener's and Botanist's Dictionary*. While waiting for these grand and ancient books to be brought to the desk, I dipped into the seventeenth-century chapter of some vast modern history of gardening. In it there was enough about this early-seventeenth-century immigrant from Italy, friend to Sir Henry Wotton and the Countess of Bedford, to make me rush back to the London Library to follow up the reference.

Lucy, Countess of Bedford, had always meant John Donne to me, and Ben Jonson. I had not realized she was a great gardener too, likely to be interested in the vegetables and fruit of Italy. It gave a whole new dimension to Jonson's punning lines:

> Lucy, you brightness of our sphere, who are
> Life of the muses' day, their morning star!

I pictured her wandering through the kitchen-garden in the sharp brightness of a summer morning, talking in Italian to this much-travelled Castelvetro about the progress of her salads and peas.

What I do remember, most vividly, is clattering up the iron stairs at the back of the London Library, to a high level I had never visited before, and coming eventually to the corner where the deep red volumes of *Italian Studies* have their home. Up there, with the sedate periodicals of so many learned societies, the solitude of the library is at its most intense. One feels completely out of time. The air is undisturbed in an awesome tranquillity of dust, held in place

Strawberries.
Giovanna Garzoni
(1600–1670)

by streaky windows and regular rows of bound volumes. It's the kingdom of philosophers and scholars. One waits, as if in an antechamber, for enlightenment. One hopes, but expects nothing.

That day I was in luck. Writing a book is for me an act of faith and folly. You have a plan of course, but you bluster about in the work, following blindly, one step after another, slogging it out in the early stages. Then suddenly you come across one thing, one reference, one passage, that explains to you why you are writing this particular book, that gives you the theme, that shows you the way. You have in a sense to earn this discovery. It is a reward. And Castelvetro was, in that sense, my reward, that voice from three hundred and sixty years ago speaking to me as if here standing beside me.

Though not directly in Italian – that came later – but through that article in *Italian Studies*, 'An Italian's message to England in 1614: Eat more fruit and vegetables'. I read through the entrancing article, not at all dead or dusty, came to the signature K. T. Butler. And realized that this was *Miss* Butler, a luminary of Newnham College when I went up to Cambridge after the war, in 1946. Her small neat figure, impeccable despite clothes rationing, had a scholarly chic that I found dazzling. She represented intellect, elegance, generosity of mind, an icon of the possibility of living a rich, rewarding life.

My last recollection of her was seeing her walk slowly away from Newnham – perhaps she was already ill, since she died in May the following year, 1950 – along Sidgwick Avenue, under the trees. I leaned on my bicycle and watched her, dimly understanding that she held knowledge that I desired, but was at that time incapable of pursuing. Then I forgot all about her. Now here in the London Library, twenty-five years later, Miss Butler was offering me more than I could have hoped for. That neat, compact figure, a study in grey, black and white in green shadows, returned to mind as clear as yesterday.

A little later, when the *Vegetable Book* was published, an old friend, Gillian Riley, told me she had seen one of the surviving MSS of Castelvetro's *Brieve racconto di tutte le radici, di tutte l'herbe et di tutti i frutti, che crudi o cotti in Italia si mangiano*, in Trinity College Library. She lent me her photocopy. She hoped at some stage to be able to work on it herself, when she could fit it into the exigencies of freelance survival, a problem we shared.

And now here it is, in Gillian Riley's fine translation that picks up the notes of crisp gaiety as well as the suppleness of Castelvetro's Italian. In great English prose of that period a tone of Biblical grandeur puts a distance between writer and reader – as do the breathless intricacies of punctuation and phrasing in lesser works such as Sir Hugh Platt's *Delights for Ladies*, as if English was not yet quite ready for describing the technicalities of life, such as gardening or sugar-boiling. Castelvetro's Italian is as lively as one could wish.

One assumes that the souls of great academics are composed of dust and old bindings (with today a nice admixture of floppy discs), but so great was Castelvetro's charm that Miss Butler fell for him. At the end of her life she tackled his other manuscripts on more elevated subjects, religion, politics, satire, discovered more about his life, his role as Italian tutor to the grand figures of the time, including James I and Anne of Denmark, his queen, his friendship with Sir Philip Sidney, Sir Henry Wotton, Sir John Harington – not, alas, the one who invented a water-closet but his cousin, brother to the Countess of Bedford. But it was in that first

1938 article that she fell in love with him, and betrays without shame or excuse – a rare thing in a scholar – her own love of good food, her own regret that the English had not taken Castelvetro's message to heart. She ends up, despairingly, with this quotation from Byron:

> But man is a carnivorous production . . .
> Although his anatomical construction
> Bears vegetables in a grumbling way,
> Your labouring people think, beyond all question,
> Beef, veal and mutton better for digestion.

I doubt whether Castelvetro was in any way concerned to touch the 'labouring people' of England. The ostensible purpose of the *Brieve racconto* is to get people here to eat more vegetables, as they do in Italy. The project is dedicated to the Countess of Bedford, a great gardener. He might expect that her circle would read it, an educated and cosmopolitan group of people who had found a hero in Prince Henry, whom it is tempting to describe as the only deeply educated member of our royal family, apart from Queen Elizabeth I and Charles I. Alas, Prince Henry, that paragon, died young, as did his close friend John Harington. Castelvetro was perhaps impatient at our slowness in absorbing the discoveries of Renaissance Italy into our eating patterns. He could see his patrons and friends building Italianate houses, planning Italian gardens, visiting Italy, speaking Italian, reading Italian writers, wearing Italian clothes. The shopping list he has left us, of things he was to bring back to friends in the north from a visit to Italy, includes soft slippers, trimmings for collars, lotions and soap, lute strings, damask from Bologna, silk flowers, perfumed gloves, masks and spectacles, as well as such edibles as caviar, botargo, tamarind and pomegranate syrup – and a long list of seeds. Perhaps he wished that as well as wearing Italian lace cuffs and smelling of Italian toilet waters, we would also sit down to the austere elegance of Italian meals with their healthy emphasis on vegetables and fruit.

Castelvetro may not have realized, moving in the circles he did, that the labouring people were indeed eating far more vegetables. It is known that Dutch Protestant settlers in the middle of the

sixteenth century brought their knowledge of intensive market gardening to Britain, especially to the areas around Norwich and Sandwich. Commentators of the time had noted this, and Miss Butler remarks on it in her 1938 study of the *Brieve racconto*. Lately this general impression has been backed up impressively with figures and statistics by Malcolm Thick, the agricultural historian. He has pointed out that the first immigrations were closely monitored and directed to certain places, that these refugees from religious persecution were extremely skilled and hardworking, and that they prospered, so that the numbers of 'strangers' grew rapidly, and to our benefit.

They were so well established around Norwich when the bad harvests of the 1590s caused a great scarcity of bread that they were able to ship quite a tonnage of root vegetables from Yarmouth to London. The shortfall in the wheat harvests greatly stimulated

*Peas and roses.
Giovanna Garzoni
(1600–1670)*

market gardening around the capital as well. In his *Profitable Instructions for the Manuring, Sowing and Planting of Kitchin Gardens*, of 1599, Richard Gardiner of Shrewsbury describes how by growing four acres of carrots and seven hundred tight-headed cabbages he was able to keep many hundreds of people going during the twenty 'pinch' days before harvest, when the previous year's wheat supply had run out.

Oddly, perhaps, carrots do not figure much in the *Brieve racconto*, but I would imagine that Castelvetro's opinion of Gardiner would be that he did not go far enough. Vegetables were not just a substitute for bread, a response to famine, but a delight in themselves. He comments that Italians do not in any case fancy meat on account of the hot climate: he does not, I think, take into account how much our climate affects our diet and how much more difficult it is for us to grow wonderful vegetables and fruit even with the intensive skills that we learned from the Dutch.

Reading Malcolm Thick's chapter on market gardening in Volume V of the *Agrarian History of England and Wales* (1985) and his more recent study on *Root Crops and the Feeding of London's Poor in the Late 16th and Early 17th Centuries* led me to itemize the vegetables Castelvetro writes about, and the fruit, to see how much was strange to gardeners in this country or unknown as imports. The answer turned out to be very little. Of the 84 varieties mentioned, 69 were being grown in this country by the end of the sixteenth century, or were regular imports (rice, olives, capers, etc.). Exotics were celery, cos lettuce, azeroles or Neapolitan medlars, the yellow bean-like lupins that one still sees in Mediterranean markets, *ovali* mushrooms, watermelons, kohlrabi, carob beans, truffles. Noteworthy absentees are Jerusalem artichokes, which had been brought back to France from Canada in 1605 or 1606, sweet potatoes (Gerard in the frontispiece of his 1597 *Herbal* is holding a sprig of potato flowers) and tomatoes (which figure in Castelvetro's shopping list of seeds but not in the *Brieve racconto*): there is no hint of peppers and chillies. He talks about varieties of millet, but omits maize – no polenta – although it figures on the shopping list as Turkish corn.

A thing that delights me in the *Brieve racconto* is the recognition of his past in our present, the continuity of small things in our civilization. Many things change: some seem to be with us for ever. When he writes of late artichokes being trimmed and thrown into a bucket of water to prevent them discolouring, I remember, on holiday in Venice on the Giudecca, passing the women who sit by the quay slicing off the leaves of artichokes into the canal, the white artichoke bottoms falling directly into a bucket. He talks of bunches of little red-cheeked sorb apples hung up on a nail to ripen, and I remember the first time Geoffrey and I ever saw them, in a little grocery in Liguria, hanging from a hook: when we ate them, they puckered the mouth.

You might conclude that Castelvetro was pushing at an open door, well a slightly open door, though it must be admitted that the gentle complaints he makes about English eating habits can still be made today so his push did not have much success (and of course it never went into print in any case). His disciple was John Evelyn, who to judge by his *Acetaria* (1699) had read the *Brieve racconto*: but then one cannot say that Evelyn had much success either in reforming our diet. Two and a half centuries later, when *Mediterranean Food* came out in 1950, Elizabeth David saw the need to say much the same things.

The English have eaten vegetables, certainly. Probably they ate vegetables in greater quantities than we have supposed. It is how they have eaten them that is the problem. In spite of centuries of tender, loving care on the part of gardeners and farmer-gardeners, they have not been given star treatment by cooks. They have not been seen as a cause of delight – apart from asparagus which we have always grown in too small quantities, whether in 1614 or last May and June. In this country I have been amazed at the way an expert gardener will tolerate the poor style in which his produce appears on the table, overcooked and watery all too often. As if delight were permissible in the garden, but not on the table.

What makes Castelvetro's *Brieve racconto* such a vivid thing for us today is his nostalgic delight in the elegant austerity of his native land. He puts me in mind of Taine, the French historian, who in the 1860s noted that the British climate leads us to meat and alcohol, which inhibits our senses and blunts our capacity to savour the pleasures of life unless we are rich enough to buy our way round the climate. "In Marseilles or Milan, a poor person can buy a pound of grapes worthy of the table of the gods, for a ha'penny, and thereby acquire the idea of exquisite sensation."

Exquisite sensation is what Castelvetro was after, from the dedication of the *Brieve racconto* to Lucy, the well-named and shining Countess of Bedford, to the happy ending over a dinner of frog's legs with a much enlightened German nobleman. He must have seen how difficult exquisite sensation is for northeners. It has nothing to do with money, feasting and lavish abundance: it was as difficult in the muddy famines of the past as it is in the sunless employment of the present. It is in the end a matter of light. Castelvetro was perhaps expressing and shaping our longing for the south, which has been defined as the place where orange trees grow out of doors in the ground rather than in tubs that have to be taken into shelter during the winter.

Light is everything. By its ferocity it imposes restraint that is the mark of the highest civilization: in exchange it gives sweetness, strength and clarity of form. The visual embodiment of the *Brieve racconto* may be seen in Giovanna Garzoni's miniature painting. Garzoni's life overlapped Castelvetro's. She too travelled about, looking for work, with Paris as her furthest destination. (She was 16 years old when he died.) When Garzoni at last settled for some years in Florence, she was able to depict fruit and vegetables – and their attendant insects – with that fine sympathy and joy that Castelvetro showed in his writing. The sensuousness is there, not in heavy contrasts of chiaroscuro, but in translucent colours and clarity of form. It is the kind of poetic, almost humorous clarity that we do not much pursue in the north. You find it in some of the best plant book illustrations of the past. For the present I can think only of Ben Nicholson. His disciplined sensuousness has nothing to do with northern self-denial, but everything to do with that southern light-filled austerity that gives such delight as we find in Castelvetro – who is at last accessible to everyone in this welcome translation.

Introduction

Giacomo Castelvetro wrote *A Brief Account of the Fruit, Herbs & Vegetables of Italy* in 1614. He was born in Modena on 25 March 1546, the son of Niccolò Castelvetro, a wealthy banker, and Liberata Tassoni, also of noble birth. He died in London in 1616, in poverty and distress.

His long and peripatetic life had been far from unhappy, however. The first of Castelvetro's many adventures began at the age of seventeen, when he and his brother were smuggled out of Modena 'in two chests on a mule'. His enthusiasm for the reformed religion made it necessary for him to flee to join his uncle Lodovico, the humanist critic and teacher, who was living in exile in Geneva. Ludovico Castelvetro's violently expressed sympathies for the Protestant cause had led to his persecution by the Roman Inquisition, and for the next seven years Giacomo shared the wandering life of this distinguished but restless man of letters, living in Geneva, Lyons, Basle, Vienna and Chiavenna, and studying Greek and Latin as well as French, German, Spanish and English.

Ludovico's formative influence on his nephew was gastronomic as well as intellectual. He had been seriously ill as a young man, perhaps due to the miseries of his protracted battle with his family to abandon the study of law for the pursuit of literature. The illness saved him from an uncongenial career, but left him with a weak digestion. For the rest of his life Ludovico ate frugal, simple meals of fruit and vegetables, without meat or wine. His nephew Giacomo was no vegetarian, but his taste for simple vegetable dishes, carefully prepared, must have developed in those early years of wanderings in Europe with his revered uncle.

Towards the end of his life Giacomo Castelvetro taught Italian at Cambridge, and a little notebook of conversations that he wrote

15

for one of his pupils still survives. Far from being the conventional phrase-book, it consists of rather rambling exchanges between gentlemen travelling with servants and companions in unspecified parts of England and Italy. The excitement of setting off on a clear, bright morning, refreshed after a comfortable night in a pleasant inn, with congenial company and entertaining conversation, shines through the almost illegible pages. Not for Castelvetro the horrors of dishonest innkeepers and insolent servants. He knew how to travel. He was friendly, but not familiar, with the staff, and adept at bringing out the best in his host – 'Retired magistrates do, indeed, make the best innkeepers . . .' Castelvetro even left for us that item most prized by biographers – his laundry list. But our concern here is with food and we must all regret that the meal the young nephew in the notebook orders for his uncle is not itemized in full – 'Little, but well cooked,' he writes, leaving the rest to our imagination. One is reminded of the impromptu salad Castelvetro describes in the section on cabbages, made by an enterprising young Frenchwoman from a freshly picked cabbage while Castelvetro and a group of young people were waiting for a meal at an inn. Was this because the inn would not normally have offered a vegetable dish? Or was this a memory of travels with his uncle, when young Giacomo would use his wits to find simple, fresh food for his dyspeptic companion?

Castelvetro was liked by all who knew him, and his pleasant disposition must have smoothed the way for the travellers when he was on the road with Ludovico, who, though ascetic and austere, had a violent temper. Many of the dialogues in the Italian conversation book concern the settling of differences between fellow guests, or servant and master.

Ludovico's health problems may well have stimulated Castelvetro's interest in diet, for he had urinary troubles as well as a weak digestion. Many of the remedies in the *Brief Account* are for such complaints.

Very little is known about Castelvetro's early years in Modena. His *Album amicorum* tells rather sourly of being a sickly child, which he blames on his mother, his only mention of this lady. He survived the alarming experience of sharing a bedroom with an old person who had the plague.

Ludovico Castelvetro, Giacomo's uncle, from L. A. Muratori, Opere varie critiche, *1727*

The descriptions of childhood pastimes, like the family ritual of the lucky draw for coins hidden in medlars, are more serene, as are his vignettes of children learning to swim on floats made out of dried pumpkins, or being sent to bed early in order to be fresh for school next morning. (How different from today!)

Castelvetro has some cheerful memories of his student days in Germany and Switzerland, such as a rather peevish outburst from a young German woman who objected to Castelvetro eating grapes while he picked them, whereas in Italy the harvesters would be glad to give them away. Or the young count who got so confused over the techniques of truffle hunting.

After his uncle's death in 1571 Castelvetro studied German for a time in Baden and then moved to England, where he taught Italian and soon found friends and patrons. He spent two years escorting the young Sir John North on an educational tour of Italy, and remembers in the *Brief Account* how they both enjoyed the hospitality of the generous Italian vineyards. Then his father's attempts to get him to stop gadding around and settle down in Modena partly succeeded when Castelvetro was obliged to return home to claim his share of the inheritance under his will. But he could not reconcile his fierce Protestantism with the need to placate the Inquisition, and he was forced to sell his share of his father's estate and return to England. Much of his bitterness

Still life with ham. Munari, seventeenth century

17

against the Roman Catholic church must stem from this second flight from his home town; wandering off as a travelling student was one thing, but having to flee for his life quite another.

When Castelvetro returned to England in the 1580s he plunged into the exhilarating literary world of Elizabethan London, and was busy promoting the use of the Italian language and active in publishing contemporary Italian literature. He mixed with other Italian intellectuals living and working in London and enjoyed the patronage of Sir Walter Ralegh and Sir Philip Sidney. He must have had ample opportunity to experience the feasting in noble households as well as the humbler fare of his expatriate neighbours in the Tower Ward, where he was living next door to Horatio Pallavicino and listed in a register of aliens as 'attending no church'.

Frequent trips to Europe followed, to the great Book Fair in Frankfurt, for example, and to Basle, where he married Isotta de' Canonici. Castelvetro's only recorded reference to her is in the Castelvetro family tree he later drew up when he was living in Edinburgh. Tommaso Sandonnini, who published the family tree in his book on the Castelvetro family in 1882, assumed that she was an unknown woman who probably died young. On the contrary, Isotta was a widow of comfortable means when she married Giacomo Castelvetro in Basle in 1587. Her first husband had been Thomas Lieber, or Erastus, the distinguished doctor and philosopher, and biographers of Castelvetro have implied that the marriage was a rather cynical piece of opportunism on his part, for it made him executor of Erastus's literary estate. In fact we know nothing at all about the relationship, but at a time when marriages were frequently business arrangements, it could well have been a most satisfactory one. Her husband had been dead for nearly four years when she remarried, and Isotta, from a noble family in Bologna, was perhaps lonely, and glad of the company of a lively, intelligent compatriot.

In London, she would have enjoyed the society of other Italians, in particular those associated with John Wolf, the printer and publisher. Castelvetro himself was enjoying perhaps the happiest and most successful period of his life, publishing and promoting Italian literature, in an atmosphere of considerable

intellectual excitement, and helping to establish his native tongue as the common language of the literati of Europe.

The vegetable stall.
Joachim Beuckelaer
(c. 1530/35–1573/4)

Castelvetro edited a collection of Erastus's medical works which was published in a handsome edition in 1590. His elegantly written Latin introduction explains candidly how, by marrying the author's widow, the editor Castelvetro acquired, *hereditario iure*, the right to publish his writings. I have been unable to discover if Castelvetro made any money out of this publication, or whether it was a labour of love, financed by Castelvetro, or more likely Isotta, as a tribute to Erastus.

Castelvetro's editorial work in preparing a manuscript of this kind for the press must have been enormous, but he would have found the task congenial. (In the last years of his life he was busy making a fair copy of a similar manuscript by the eighty-seven-year-old Taddeo Duni of Zürich.) So the marriage could have been a reasonable arrangement for all parties: a responsible handling of Erastus's literary estate, a husband and a change of scene for Isotta and a comfortably off wife and companion for

Pears and cherries.
Giovanna Garzoni
(1600–1670)

Castelvetro. That she was held in some esteem in London can be inferred from the inscription in a curious little book in the British Library, a critical account of Jewish medicine printed in 1570 with an inscription on the title-page in the hand of Dr Gabriel Harvey: 'This very book sent to the famous doctor Erastus, by Dr Struppius. Given me by Mistris Castelvetro, late wife of Erastus'.

In 1592 Castelvetro realized at last the ambition he had nursed for six years, to be Italian tutor to James VI of Scotland. Edinburgh may have been a welcome change from the competitiveness of Elizabethan London, where, I suspect, Castelvetro was no match for the ruthless entrepreneurial characters on the make in the Italian studies field. Years later Queen Anne of Denmark, James's consort, was complimented on her fluent Italian, and her familiarity with Guarini's *Pastor fido*, which Castelvetro had published in London in 1591, so his teaching must have been a success. No doubt it was Queen Anne who gave him an introduction to the court of Denmark, where he went in 1594, after the death of his wife.

Isotta's will left her household goods in Edinburgh, and some valuables, to Castelvetro, and the bulk of her estate to relatives in

Basle. This was a not unreasonable division of her first husband's estate, but it must have left Castelvetro with diminished resources, although with the freedom to set off again on his wanderings.

We catch up with him next in Sweden, on friendly terms with Duke Charles (who became king in 1599), with whom he shared a passion for gardening. Together they grafted scions from a fine pear tree, which Castelvetro had preserved in a pot of honey, on to a tree in the Duke's private garden.

Castelvetro was passionately concerned with contemporary politics, particularly the confrontations between Roman Catholic and Protestant states. Throughout his life he devoted much time and energy to getting hold of first-hand accounts of diplomatic and political events and copying out his versions of them, which were by no means objective, coruscating with virulent anti-Catholic sentiments. His role as Italian master in various royal households must have been useful here, giving him access to correspondence and ambassadors' reports, and making it easy to gather and pass on information.

Some of this anti-Catholicism shows in the *Brief Account* when Castelvetro speaks disparagingly of the belief in purgatory, knowing that his views would be shared by the Countess of Bedford, for whom he wrote the book, and her circle.

Some writers have been quick to assume that, since Castelvetro was at one time on Sir Robert Cecil's payroll, he must have been a spy for the English government during his travels around Europe, but what we know of his engagingly open and indiscreet personality makes this seem extremely unlikely. A competent spy would hardly be expected to leave neatly written documents all over the place, with his name and that of his informants carefully appended.

A collection of some of these political papers is now in the Newberry Library in Chicago. These may well be the ones Castelvetro mentions in his notebook, which he left with friends in Copenhagen, probably as security for a loan, on his return to Italy in 1598.

In May of that year Castelvetro said goodbye to his royal friends and set off on a leisurely journey through Europe, staying with acquaintances in France, Switzerland and Germany. He started a

notebook, an *Album amicorum*, in which he recorded details of his journey, the names of the friends he stayed with, and a list of Italian luxuries to send back to Sweden. It included cheeses and sausages from Bologna and Modena, preserved figs, pomegranate wine, spices from Venice, embroidered gloves, fine writing paper and over sixty books, as well as an alphabetical list of plants and seeds.

The journey stretched over several months, with visits to the fairs of Frankfurt, Ulm, Nuremberg and Augsburg. By the end of 1599 Castelvetro had settled in Venice, where he worked for the publisher G. B. Ciotto, editing and preparing manuscripts of contemporary Italian poetry and fiction, and was much appreciated for his sane, firm approach.

He was on good terms with the English ambassador, Sir Henry Wotton, teaching Italian to visiting foreigners and translating and circulating political papers. Memories of these years in the *Brief Account* are of delicious asparagus from Verona, boatloads of wine from Modena, the green shade from beans planted by Venetian women in their window boxes.

Nearly twelve years of busy, congenial activity came to an abrupt end in 1611 when the Inquisition imprisoned Castelvetro, after being tipped off by an informer whose corpse turned up floating in a canal a few days later. Castelvetro's anti-papal activities had always been wildly indiscreet and the mass of papers in his rooms would have incriminated him beyond any hope of release. The first thing the new English ambassador, Sir Dudley Carleton, did when he heard of Castelvetro's incarceration was to rush and grab all the papers he could find before the Inquisition got hold of them. Carleton was an ambitious young career diplomat, not at all pleased with his posting to Venice, which was something of a political backwater. He was bored and exasperated by the trivialities of his duties: dispatching a consignment of Venetian glass for Lady Cope, who scolded him for not choosing sufficiently ornate samples; having to find lodgings for stranded tourists . . . Castelvetro's imprisonment gave him a chance to show his mettle and he made the most of it, acting with tact and firmness. The Venetian Senate was persuaded that the arbitrary arrest of a member of the diplomatic household, at one time a

Opposite:
Still life (detail).
Rachel Ruysch,
(1664–1750)

Sir Dudley Carleton.
M. van Mieteveldt,
c. *1620*

23

servant of the English king (James VI of Scotland had by now succeeded to the throne of England), could become an international incident. The Senate was not unwilling to be seen resisting the interference of the Papacy in its internal affairs. Castelvetro was freed, but on condition that he left Venice at once.

If he had gone straight to London, where his misfortunes had aroused so much sympathy among his friends in politics and publishing, he would surely have found a patron and employment. But Castelvetro set off yet again on a round of visits to friends and colleagues on the Continent, and by the time he eventually arrived in London in 1613 the incident was no longer fresh in people's minds.

Only Sir John Harington, one of the young men to whom he had taught Italian in Venice, responded to Castelvetro's cry for help. He gave him an annual pension of £5, but this was paid for only one year, for Harington died in 1614.

Castelvetro taught Italian for a term at Cambridge University but failed to find any other source of income. In 1614 he was living in the household of Sir Adam Newton at Eltham Park and later in that year moved with the family to their sumptuous new mansion at Charlton, near Greenwich. Sir Adam Newton had been tutor to Prince Henry, a close friend of John Harington. He was married to the daughter of Sir John Puckering, the Lord Chancellor, and was later to become treasurer to King Charles I. It is hard to understand why Castelvetro seemed to be unhappy in this wealthy, intellectual household. Perhaps because, although lodged and fed, and on familiar terms with the family, as the anecdote about the mushroom in Eltham Park implies, he lacked dignified employment and an income. Entries in his *Album* note his poor health and dire financial situation. On New Year's Eve 1614 Castelvetro writes that for once he had really enjoyed his dinner, and that he had had to borrow five shillings from a friend to buy some wax candles and pay his shoemaker and the French copyist (perhaps the one who wrote out the manuscript of *A Brief Account*). Twelve months later he made the last entry in his *Album*, as legible and vividly expressed as ever. He was still troubled with gout and rheumatism and recovering from attacks of fever and asthma which left him so weak he had to walk with a stick. Short of

Calamaro

money for necessities and bothered by the lice in his coat, Castelvetro nevertheless continued to hope that the king or the City of London might perhaps reward him for the translation he had made the previous year of James's treatise on kingship. He hoped in vain, and died, probably at Charlton, in 1616. One of his last letters was to a friend in Venice asking for various vegetable seeds and some spices.

It was at Charlton that Castelvetro wrote the *Brief Account of the Fruit, Herbs & Vegetables of Italy* and dedicated it to Lucy, Countess of Bedford. It was natural that Castelvetro should turn, in his need for support, to Lucy, the sister of Sir John Harington, his former pupil and patron described in his funeral oration as 'temperate in feeding, rare in feasting and frequent in fasting'.

Beautiful and intelligent, the countess was known and loved for her generous support of writers and poets. She was one of the more dazzling members of the court of Queen Anne of Denmark, and through her marriage to Edward Russell, third Earl of Bedford, enjoyed the friendship of some of the most powerful politicians and courtiers of the day. Like Castelvetro, she had an enthusiasm for gardening and her house at Twickenham was planned with a fine vegetable garden and formal arrangements of trees and grass. But above all Lucy appeared to the world to be extremely wealthy. Unfortunately for Castelvetro, however, Lucy's father, Lord Harington of Exton, had died in 1613, leaving his son John vast estates, but also enormous debts, accumulated during Lord Harington's wardship of Princess Elizabeth, the daughter of James I. His son did his best to disentangle the confusion, but died a few months later, and his sister Lucy in her turn inherited debts of what would today be about £4m.

Lucy and her husband already had money problems of their own and she was now in dire financial straits, but few of her contemporaries realized that and at least ten writers dedicated works to her. John Donne sent an elegy on the death of her brother and a plea for help with his debts. A close friend of Lucy, he received £30. The friendship just about survived, but Donne looked elsewhere for official patronage. Castelvetro, who could have managed on his previous pension of £5, got nothing. If the appeal had come two years earlier, before Lucy's financial situa-

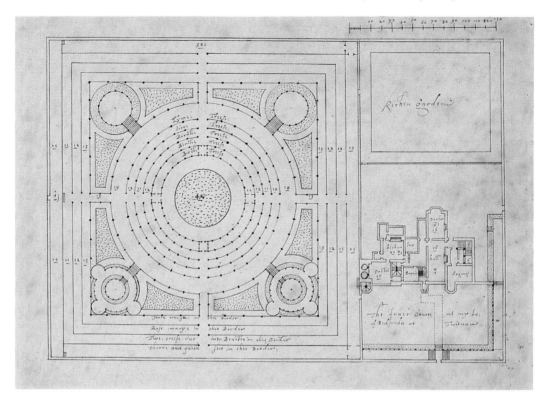

Plan of the garden of the Countess of Bedford's house at Twickenham Park. Drawing by Robert Smythson, c. 1609

tion had deteriorated, Castelvetro might well have had a happier old age.

Lucy was married to Edward Russell when she was almost fourteen years old. Although this was an arranged marriage they seem to have been happy together. The glamour and prestige of her position in the influential Russell family must have compensated Lucy for the somewhat bland qualities of her husband. After his rather bumbling participation in the Earl of Essex's unsuccessful rebellion against Elizabeth I, he retired to his estate at Chenies in Buckinghamshire, chastened by a fine of £20,000, and settled down contentedly to a rural existence, hunting and managing his various properties. Meanwhile his brilliant young wife pursued her career at court.

Intelligent, well-educated, energetic and ambitious, Lucy certainly needed an outlet for her talents. She spent the last quarter of each year as lady-in-waiting to the queen and was involved in many of the entertainments and spectacles of the court. She flung

26

herself into the production of masques, extravagant multi-media entertainments, heady mixtures of pageant, drama, music and dance, in which professional actors and singers as well as courtiers took part. There was scope for serious poetry, heavy with allegory and symbolism, and plenty of fun and feasting for the less intellectual. The audience participated in the dancing; Lucy's serious young brother, John, was one of the leading performers. By all accounts Lucy thoroughly enjoyed the dancing and dressing-up, and spent recklessly on the jewelled costumes she wore to such advantage.

In *The Masque of Queenes*, which was performed in 1609 at a cost of £3,000, Lucy was resplendent as Penthesilea, Queen of the Amazons, in a costume designed by Inigo Jones with a head-dress which managed to combine a cascade of feathers, jewels, a helmet and a crown, and a bodice which was either immodestly see-through or a voluptuously moulded imitation of one of the less practical suits of ceremonial armour.

Lucy's more sober pursuits included a passionate interest in literature and poetry. The writers whose company she enjoyed were grateful for her criticism and encouragement as well as her financial support. John Florio, an Italian contemporary and friend of Castelvetro, was living in Lucy's house while working on his translation of Montaigne's *Essays* and referred wrily in his dedication to her firmness in keeping him at it and her warmth and kindness: '. . . to put and keep me in heart like a captived cannibal fattened against my death, you often cried *coraggio* and called *ça ça*, and applauded as I passed'.

Lucy spoke and wrote fluent Italian and it would have been inappropriate for Castelvetro to have addressed her in any other language. He was respected as an authority on the literature and grammar of his native tongue and Lucy would have appreciated the deceptive simplicity of the style of his *Brief Account of the Fruit, Herbs & Vegetables of Italy*.

The costume designed by Inigo Jones for the Countess as Penthesilea, Queen of the Amazons

Castelvetro wrote his book on fruit and vegetables in an attempt to persuade the English to improve their diet by eating less meat and more fruit and vegetables. He gently criticizes us for eating too many sweet things and over-rich dishes, and for not making a more imaginative use of the plants and vegetables introduced from abroad, like artichokes and aubergines. Careful to avoid a dogmatic or hectoring tone, Castelvetro sets about our conversion with a seductive account of the fruit and vegetables of his beloved homeland, describing them as they come into season, from the delights of asparagus in spring to the comforts of chestnut and cabbage stew in winter.

Castelvetro did not intend to write a recipe book. He must have known the works of Vicenzo Cervio, Bartolomeo Scappi and Giovanni Rosselli, describing the elaborate banquets of the courts of the Italian nobility, and felt passionately about a very different gastronomy. He did not attempt to disparage the food of the rich, for he needed their patronage. But with tact and good humour Castelvetro expounded his own ideas of luxury – exquisitely fresh vegetables, simply prepared, using the finest ingredients. This was as far from the basic subsistence food of the poor as from the rich, elaborate dishes of the household of the d'Este and Gonzagas, or our own James I.

He does give recipes when necessary, to explain how to use a particular fruit or vegetable, but the simple approach is what Castelvetro wanted to get across. The basic method for so many dishes could hardly be called a recipe: cook your vegetables simply in salted water and serve them tepid or cold with oil, salt and pepper and bitter orange or lemon juice.

An alternative method for cabbages, celery or root vegetables is equally simple: cook them first in water or stock, then finish them in a rich stock, thicken the dish with breadcrumbs or beaten egg and serve them hot, seasoned with pepper, spices or cheese.

Castelvetro suggests subtle variations on these two themes, adding a little raw onion to the salad of uncooked purslane, just as I am told to do by my local Turkish greengrocer; or cooking his broccoli with a few chopped cloves of garlic, a magic touch, which transforms the dish, whether eaten hot with cheese and pepper, or cold with oil and lemon juice.

A third way of cooking vegetables is to roast them over hot coals, or in the ashes, wrapped in damp paper, which is not possible in most domestic kitchens, but is ideal for barbecues. Root vegetables like carrots and parsnips are good cooked over charcoal, and leafy ones like cabbage and lettuce hearts are delicious served with good olive oil and a squeeze of bitter orange juice. Recently many health-conscious northern Italian restaurants have taken to serving a plate of charcoal-grilled vegetables as an alternative to a main meat course.

Nowhere does Castelvetro tell us to cook vegetables *al dente*. This unsubtle practice works quite well for some vegetables like broccoli, cauliflower or mangetout peas, but anyone who has chomped their way through an exquisite arrangement of virtually raw items will appreciate that many vegetables are best when properly cooked. Take cabbage – Castelvetro tells us to plunge a whole, washed head of cabbage, still on its stalk, into a pot of

Still life.
Neapolitan school,
seventeenth century

Overleaf:
The fruit seller.
Vicenzo Campi
(1536–91)

29

Still life with
guinea-fowl.
Munari,
seventeenth century

boiling water for a few minutes. Other varieties of cabbage need to be well-cooked, simmered slowly in good broth with aromatics and lumps of bacon.

Castelvetro was by no means a vegetarian. Many of his recipes need good, rich broth, which would have been the by-product of some of the gross meat dishes he avoids mentioning. (In Castelvetro's text I translate *brodo* as broth rather than stock to avoid association with commercial stock cubes, coarsely flavoured and reinforced with MSG.) Some dishes require the addition of hard bacon fat, creamed with herbs and garlic, a seasoning still used in bean and lentil dishes today. But the food eaten in Lent and on the 'lean' days prescribed by the church would make perfect vegan dishes. Meat and dairy produce were not allowed, so olive oil and almond milk and almond butter were used to give richness to fish and vegetable dishes.

The vegetable dishes where meat is absent or appears only in small amounts, as a garnish rather than the main ingredient, are very much to our taste. Vegetable purées as a filling for pies and tarts are similar to the delicious Middle Eastern pastries which were once part of Europe's Moorish inheritance and are now happily being rediscovered. Many of Castelvetro's recipes for

32

little pastries using pasta dough or shortcrust pastry are delicious made with *fila* pastry.

Where a plant has medicinal properties that can be applied simply and effectively, Castelvetro explains them. His interest in the connection between diet and health was considerable, and he seems to have had first-hand experience of helping sick friends with potions and remedies, as well as his professional work in preparing medical manuscripts for the press. But Castelvetro never becomes pompous or tedious, and this lightness of touch must make him unique among his contemporaries. He even manages to make references to the four humours seem comprehensible.

The doctrine of the four humours was still, in the late sixteenth century, the basis of medical theory. All humans, animals and plants are made up of different proportions of the basic elements – fire, earth, air and water. Their temperaments, health and general behaviour are formed by the balance of these elements. A person, or a substance, can be hot, cold, wet or dry (sanguine, saturnine, melancholic, choleric), in varying degrees. Any disturbance of this balance results in disease or illness. Health can be restored by correcting this imbalance. Good health can be maintained by watching what you eat and making sure no imbalance occurs. What you eat, how you cook it, what sauces you serve with it, depends on your humour or temperament. The theory of the humours gave plenty of scope for the moralist in the kitchen and can make extremely tedious reading. One of Castelvetro's many virtues is that he trips deftly among the humours, without letting his narrative get bogged down with them. Pepper, he tells us, is the best seasoning for beans, without, mercifully, going on to explain that beans are warm and wet in the first degree, and therefore need to be balanced with pepper, which is dry in the third degree.

The application of the theory of humours in the kitchen and the stillroom was really a matter of commonsense. Redcurrant jelly with venison, our own malt vinegar with fish and chips, Castelvetro's bitter orange juice with buttered pumpkin, are all ways of balancing the different qualities of food. A food that is 'cold' and 'wet', like fish, needs a nice green sauce of pounded

The sober fast. G. M. Mitelli (1634–1718)

IL CARNEVAL PAZZO

The crazy carnival. G. M. Mitelli (1634–1718)

Poma amoris fructu
rubro.

Tomato. Coloured engraving in Basilius Besler, Hortus Eystettensis, *1613*

Piper Indicum maxi‚
mum longum‚.

Piper Indicum minus
recurvis siliquis.

Chilli. Coloured engraving in Basilius Besler, Hortus Eystettensis, *1613*

herbs, mainly parsley, which is 'warm' and 'dry'. Women caring for the health of a large establishment would have a store of such precepts and remedies handed down from mothers and grand-mothers, sometimes written out in notebooks, and passed on to future generations. Lucy, Countess of Bedford, cared for her large household in the same way, and certainly would not have needed to have the theory of the humours spelt out to her.

The theory could be somewhat heavy going as expounded in sixteenth- and seventeenth-century treatises on food and plants. For example Baldassare Pisanelli's treatise *On the Nature of Food and Drink* is full of interesting information about the qualities of different foods and their antidotes, but is not mouthwatering when it comes to recipes. One suspects a great divide between the doctors and the cooks, and appreciates Castelvetro all the more for the elegance with which he bridges the gap between the two. His recipes are written with the ease and grace of someone who is as at home in the kitchen as in the study. He does not pontificate or make a great fuss, just tells us simply how to make a nice dish from the vegetable or fruit he is describing.

The same goes for his gardening information. Castelvetro tells us how to earth up celery or plant an asparagus bed, and we sense that he knows just what he is talking about. He had the wit and modesty to write unpretentiously about things he knew and loved, and this shines through the manuscript, even when he gets carried away by the awfulness of German salads, when his sentences splutter and unroll like unresolved cadenzas.

Castelvetro's message appeals to us today because of its emphasis on freshness and simplicity, the two great qualities of Italian cooking. But we should not forget that the Italian kitchen in Castelvetro's time was very different from the one we know now.

As I strolled round Modena, Castelvetro's birthplace, one Sunday morning, I reflected how strange and outlandish the aromas would have been to its native son. Of the freshly roasted coffee in the bars, the *cappuccino* perfumed with a sprinkling of chocolate, the crisp, freshly baked pastries powdered with vanilla sugar and pizzas glowing with tomatoes and peppers, only the oregano and garlic would have had their place in Castelvetro's kitchen.

Some of today's best-loved ingredients would have been unknown in the late sixteenth century. Tomatoes were indigestible curiosities, reared for show in the private gardens of the rich. Chillies would have made a pretty sight in pots, but their explosive potential was yet to be realized. Potatoes were still a novelty. Only some varieties of beans seem to have taken off, those Castelvetro describes as '*nostrano*' (native), as opposed to the 'Turkish', meaning exotic.

Modena came up with food that would have been familiar to Castelvetro, though: ravioli with a filling of pumpkin purée flavoured with *amaretti*, and *bollito misto*, a succulent assortment of boiled meats, including a tasty pig's cheek and a *cotechino*, chicken, pickled tongue, beef and ham, simmered in a rich, aromatic broth, and served with a sauce of green herbs pounded with olive oil, anchovies, capers and balsamic vinegar.

To eat in the style of Castelvetro we would have to banish from our larders tomatoes, chillies, sweet peppers and potatoes, and also the aromatics vanilla, cocoa and coffee; dried fruit and pots of jam should be pushed to the back of the shelf. We should eat fresh fruit instead of cooked puddings and disregard all the beguiling snacks and titbits he dismisses as fit only for 'pregnant women and silly children'. Sugar should be restored to its ancient role of condiment, and used to accentuate other flavours rather than as a sweetener. A sprinkling of spices might perfume dishes towards the end of cooking, sharpness being added with fresh bitter orange or lemon juice rather than vinegar or pickles. Light fruity sauces based on gooseberries or unripe grapes would replace heavy gravies and cream-based sauces.

It is difficult to discover if Castelvetro's criticisms of English cooking were entirely justified. Recipe books of the period did not, on the whole, describe things people knew all about already, or took for granted. The vegetable dishes that may well have accompanied the gross meat dishes he so disliked never got written about. The handwritten cookery notebooks, of which a surprising number survive, do not tell us about the simple, everyday dishes that women prepared as a matter of course. But the recipes they do describe give us some idea of what was new, interesting or unfamiliar to the seventeenth-century housewife.

Still life (detail).
D. de Heem,
seventeenth
century

Elinor Fettiplace, who compiled one of these notebooks around 1604, was from the lesser gentry of Oxfordshire and Gloucestershire. In Hilary Spurling's recreation of Elinor's gastronomic year we can enjoy a collection of elegant recipes, rather thin on vegetable dishes, but indicating a new taste for light, delicately flavoured food. There are lovely light creams and puddings, very different from the traditional 'Christmas Pies' Castelvetro found so inordinately full of rich, dried fruit. She uses artichokes in pies or a cream sauce, which are every bit as imaginative as Castelvetro's recipes. There are two delicious, subtle recipes for spinach, one of them a tart, where dried fruit and sugar are used sparingly, to flavour rather than sweeten.

If this taste was widespread, Castelvetro may have been preaching to the converted, and Lucy, Countess of Bedford, would already be enjoying the new cuisine. Castelvetro, remembering in his old age the rich banquets of the Elizabethan court, or the heavy food of northern Europe, and homesick for the sights and aromas of his beloved Italy, may have been unaware of the changes going on around him in 1614, particularly if Lady Newton, in whose house he was living when he wrote his *Brief Account*, was not an imaginative housekeeper.

The food of the poor, in England as in Italy, would have been another matter. The more humble legumes, such as grass peas and chickpeas, were dismissed by Castelvetro as fit only for the lowest of the low. He mentions the supplies of millet and chestnuts kept in reserve in the state fortresses of the Venetian Republic, for the relief of famine in times of war. For many this would have been staple food, if they were lucky. The miseries of famine and disease were never far from everyone's minds, and the still-life paintings which glow with an abundance and excess of edible riches are, from the market scenes of Valckenborsch to the miniatures of Giovanna Garzoni, statements about the wealth of the owner of the painting and talismans to repel the spectres of dearth and want. The dried cannabis branches which Castelvetro recommends to grow beans up were probably the by-product of a crop used medicinally to dull the aches of hunger and pain felt by the poor. The diseases of malnutrition or the illnesses caused by adulterated or spoiled foodstuffs were widespread, and though

they do not figure in Castelvetro's manuscript, he must have seen plenty of them on his travels.

Castelvetro was not the first to write an essay on salads and vegetables. Alongside the serious works of the great botanists, manuscript letters circulated between enthusiasts. Castelvetro may have come across a copy of *Lettera sulle insalate* written in 1567 by Costanzo Felici of Piobbico for his friend Ulisse Aldrovandi, the great collector of plants and professor of Botany

The fruit seller ('The rotten apple injures its neighbour'). Joachim Wttwael (1566–1638)

at Bologna University. This is a loving account of the herbs and plants Felici grew or gathered in the little town of Piobbico where he practised as a doctor. He quotes with enthusiasm the proverb: '*L'insalata ben salata, poco aceto e ben oliata*', which Castelvetro says is the fundamental law of salad-making. Like Castelvetro, he also writes of children learning to swim strapped to dried pumpkins, but we should not assume from this that Castelvetro took the idea for his own essay from Felici's manuscript.

Castelvetro, although a distinguished linguist and man of letters, was no botanist, and his own essay has all the inaccuracies and misnomers of an enthusiastic amateur.

Sincerity and spontaneity are characteristics of Castelvetro's style which appeal to us today. After battling with the sixty-eight chapters of Salvatore Massonio's work on salads, *Archidipno overo dell'insalata*, a tome of monumental tedium published in 1627, enlivened only by the description of a long-dead scorpion impaled on the fork of the unfortunate author, one appreciates all the more Castelvetro's deceptively simple, almost conversational tone of voice.

John Evelyn's *Acetaria, a Discourse of Sallets*, of 1699, is a much more pretentious work, with the statutory references to the four humours and copious quotations from classical authors. There is a sort of whimsical tone to Evelyn, writing in a mock-heroic style about an amusingly rustic subject. But Castelvetro wrote with modesty and sincerity about something he cared passionately about, with the occasional old-fashioned turn of phrase of an old man using the idiom of his youth, rather than a scholar displaying his erudition.

Castelvetro may have first thought of writing his work on vegetables during the years he was living in the cold climate of northern Europe. The first pages of the notebook Castelvetro started when he set off on the long journey back to Italy from Sweden in 1598 contain an alphabetical list of seeds and plants, part of his amazing shopping list of Italian luxuries for the royal family. This list reads like an index to the work Castelvetro was to write sixteen years later. Perhaps his original idea had been to convert the Swedes to the refinements of Italian gastronomy, and it seemed worth while resurrecting it for his appeal to the Countess of Bedford.

Zamer Hanff.

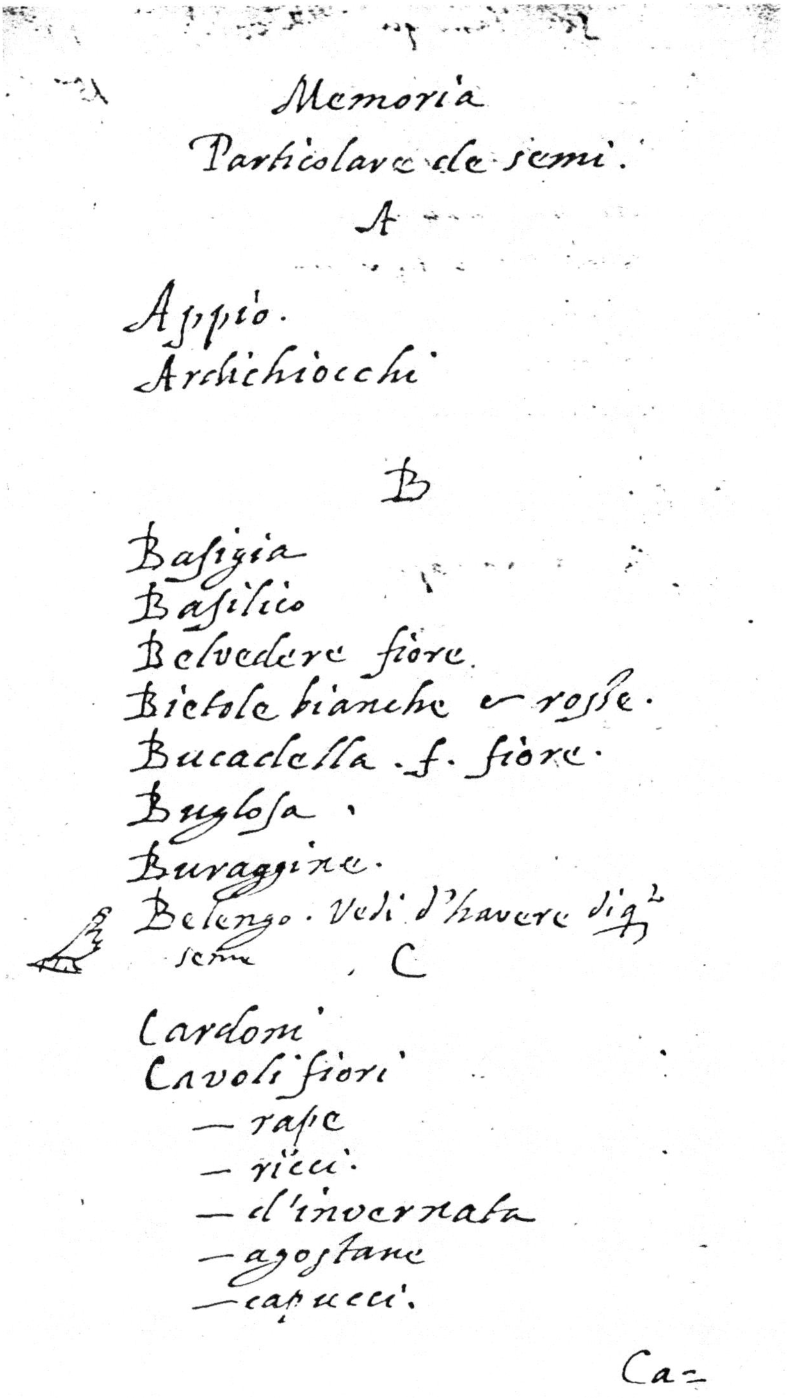

Memoria
Particolare de semi.
A

Appio.
Archichiocchi

B

Basigia
Basilico
Belvedere fiore.
Bietole bianche e rosse.
Bucadella . f. fiore.
Buglosa .
Buraggine.
Belengo. Vedi d'havere dig.²
semi , C

Cardoni
Cavoli fiori
— rape
— ricci
— d'invernata
— agostane
— capucci.

Ca =

Part of the list of seeds Castelvetro wrote in his Album amicorum

43

Plums, jasmine, walnuts and convolvulus. Giovanna Garzoni (1600–1670)

It is tempting to speculate what life would have been like for Castelvetro if that appeal had been made at a more propitious time, for Lucy would have been the ideal patron. He would have been a useful and respected member of her household at Moor Park in Hertfordshire, happily busy with advice and practical help in the design of the new Italian garden; full of concern and remedies for her husband's infirmities; active in the management of the library; and no doubt popping in and out of the kitchen. It is tragic that through sheer bad timing he lost the chance of a comfortable and respected old age, and died instead in less happy circumstances.

But it is fortunate for us that at last we can read Castelvetro's message, as timely now as it was over three and a half centuries ago, and enjoy the pleasures of cooking and eating some of the fruit and vegetables of his beloved Italy.

A
Brief Account
of the
Fruit, Herbs & Vegetables
of Italy

All'Ill.ma S.ra S.ra et Padrona Osser.ma

La S.ra Lucia Contessa di

Bedford.

Dedication

To my most illustrious lady & patron,
Lucy, Countess of Bedford

God, in His wisdom, held me worthy of being of service in teaching Italian to your Ladyship's late brother, Sir John Harington. I venture today to beseech His Divine Majesty to admit me to the company of your Ladyship's most faithful servants.

As your Ladyship must know, I was imprisoned by the Inquisition two years ago in Venice. God rescued me from its murderous clutches through the intervention of His Majesty's Ambassador, who dispatched me to safety here in England. When I arrived, I was courteously received by my former patron, your Ladyship's brother. As soon as he heard of my impoverished condition, he instructed that I should be given a pension, which was duly paid, as his Lordship's faithful overseer Monsieur Purefoy well knows. My late patron also endeavoured to procure for me a comfortable and honourable situation by which I need not be a burden to anyone, thanks to the talents the Good Lord endowed me with.

I therefore beseech your Ladyship most earnestly that if the occasion ever arises she should do the same, to the everlasting honour and prosperity of her name. Meanwhile I hope she will not disdain to accept this humble offering, compiled at the request of my Lord her brother; her well-known enthusiasm for all matters concerning the health and well-being of mankind may dispose her to consider it of some small interest. I humbly salute your Ladyship and kiss your hand.

London, the 27th of July 1614.

Your Ladyship's most humble & obedient servant,

Giac.° Castelvetri.

Fennel and parsley.
Platearius,
Livre des simples
médecines

Spring

I often reflect upon the variety of good things to eat which have been introduced into this noble country of yours over the past fifty years. The vast influx of so many refugees from the evils and cruelties of the Roman Inquisition has led to the introduction of delights previously considered inedible, worthless or even poisonous. Yet I am amazed that so few of these delicious and health-giving plants are being grown to be eaten. Through ignorance or indifference, it seems to me that they are cultivated less for the table than for show by those who want to boast of their exotic plants and well-stocked gardens.

This moves me to write down all I can remember of the names of the herbs, fruits and plants we eat in Italy, my civilized homeland, and to explain how to prepare them, either raw or cooked, for the table, so that the English no longer need be deprived through lack of information of the delights of growing and eating them.

I shall therefore begin my, I trust not unworthy, undertaking, with God's blessing and an ardent wish to give pleasure to my fellow men, by describing the first fruits of our green and pleasant spring time.

Hops I start with hops, the first shoots to appear at this time of year. We never eat them raw, but serve them as a cooked salad. We wash the hops thoroughly and then cook the desired amount in water with a little salt, drain them very well and serve them in a clean dish seasoned with salt, plenty of oil and a little vinegar or lemon juice and some crushed, not powdered, pepper.

Alternatively, once the hops are cooked, we flour them and fry them in oil and serve them sprinkled with salt, pepper and bitter orange juice.*

Hops are an excellent herb for refreshing and purifying the blood. So those of us who are concerned about our health but do not wish to bother the doctor with trivial complaints, or fall into the hands of some grasping druggist, take a handful of hops and the same amount of fumitory, endive and borage, and boil them, well washed, in fresh water without salt. There should be at least two quarts of liquid which must be boiled until reduced by half. The leaves are then taken out and eaten as a salad. The following morning, on rising, we drink a glass of the liquid, tepid, and continue thus for seven to nine days. We then take a dose of senna or manna, or some other light purgative. In this way, we keep ourselves fresh and healthy at very small cost. This medicine is particularly good for any unpleasant itching rash, which it clears up rapidly.

Spinach Next comes spinach, a very good and wholesome garden plant, which we eat on its own or accompanied by other herbs, such as spinach beets, parsley and borage.

In Italy it is eaten especially in Lent, cooked in salted water and served with oil, pepper, a little verjuice and raisins.

Another way is to cook the spinach first in plain water, drain it, chop it very fine with a large knife, and finish cooking it on a low

*The Glossary gives further information on many of the ingredients mentioned by Castelvetro.

heat in a pan with oil or butter, seasoned with salt, pepper and raisins; this makes a really delicious dish.

We often put this spinach mixture in tarts, and in *tortelli* which are fried in oil or butter and served with honey or, better still, sugar.

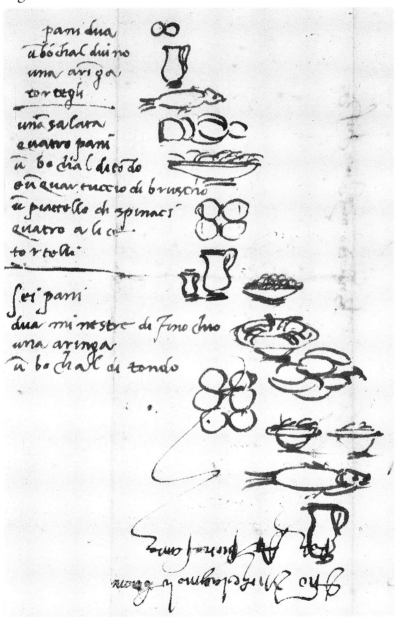

Michelangelo wrote this list of frugal meals on the back of a letter in 1517. It includes stewed fennel and a dish of spinach

Still life with asparagus. Adriaen Coorte, 1696

Next, or more or less at the same time, asparagus begins to appear, which is even better than hops as a vegetable or medicine. Some people eat it raw, with salt, pepper and Parmesan cheese, but I prefer it cooked and served like hops, with oil, a little vinegar, and salt and pepper.

Others take the plumpest spears of asparagus and having oiled them well, roll them on a plate in salt and pepper to season them thoroughly, and roast them on a grid. Lavishly sprinkled with bitter orange juice, this makes a most delicate dish.

Quite apart from being good to eat, asparagus is a most health-giving vegetable; it cannot harm any part of the human body and is positively helpful to those who find urinating painful.

At this point I shall digress a little, to explain the best method of growing asparagus, for when I see the weedy specimens of this noble plant for sale in London I never cease to wonder why no one has yet taken the trouble to improve its cultivation. It would certainly be profitable. (One really has to admire those who manage to get rich without endangering their immortal souls, for although we all acknowledge that the pursuit of disproportionate profits is a sin, it surely offends neither the Good Lord nor one's neighbour to earn as comfortable a living as possible from the land.) I am convinced that with the right care you could grow abundant crops of asparagus here with spears as thick as one's middle finger, so that one acre of land would yield more income in less time than ten fields sown with wheat. I cannot pass by this opportunity to expound the best way of doing this.

First dig a ditch in the spot where you wish to grow the asparagus, say twenty feet long and ten feet wide and three feet deep. Put the soil from it to one side, and sift it carefully to remove stones and pebbles. Cover the bottom of this ditch with a layer of horns from bulls or heifers and over these a layer of the prepared earth four fingers deep. Then on top of this, plant or sow the asparagus and sprinkle over it some fragments of horn left over from the manufacture of combs or post-horns; cover this with some more

Asparagus

How to get a large crop of good thick asparagus

of the earth. If this is done in the spring, the ditch should be left half full until the following autumn, when half the remaining earth should be thrown in. Then nothing more needs to be done, apart from keeping it free from weeds.

If you want really thick asparagus, on no account cut any at all for the first two years after planting, or the third year if they were grown from seed. Cover them well in mid autumn with stable straw, which you remove when the danger of frost has passed, and then hoe the surface gently to help the young shoots to find their way out.

When cutting asparagus the shoots should never be severed above the ground, but a good finger's breadth below. Do not take the very small ones, but leave them to grow until the seeds are almost ripe, then cut the haulms and throw them away. And note also that your precious crop should never be harvested before the third year, if grown from seed, but if grown from shoots it may be cut after the second year. This long interval deters many from growing asparagus, yet they will be quite happy to plant a walnut tree and wait as long as ten years for results.

Finally, as I should have mentioned earlier, sow your asparagus seeds in rich soil in a sunny spot, with the addition of some mature, well-sieved compost, and you should get an even more copious crop. You can believe me that an asparagus bed made in this way will last a good ten to twelve years with no further attention. The roots, though, will spread unbelievably, so they should be cut back every so often, as all good gardeners know.

Whoever reads this little book should note how the landowners of Verona gave up cultivating flax and wheat some twenty years ago, realizing what large profits could be made from asparagus, and now get three times their yearly income, sending vast quantities as far as Venice, fifty miles away.

Sprouting broccoli Next come the tender shoots which grow on the stalks of cabbage or cauliflower plants left in the garden over the winter. They are cooked and served cold with oil and salt and pepper, as I described for hops. Some prefer to cook them with a few cloves of garlic, which gives them a wonderful flavour.

In Italy our artichoke season is in the spring, unlike England, where you are fortunate enough to have them all the year round.

Artichokes

We eat them raw or cooked. When they are about the size of a walnut they are good raw, with just salt, pepper and some mature cheese to bring out the flavour. Some people do not eat artichokes with cheese; they either dislike cheese, or it gives them catarrh, or they are simply unaware of how it improves the flavour. Artichokes are not so good to eat raw when they have grown as big as apples.

We cook them in your English manner, which is not to be despised, and in other ways as well.

If you do not feel like eating artichokes raw, select some small ones and cut off the tips of the pointed outer leaves. Boil them first in fresh water to take away the bitterness, and then finish cooking them in rich beef or chicken broth. Serve them in a shallow dish on slices of bread moistened with just a little of the broth, sprinkled with grated mature cheese and pepper to bring out their goodness. We love these tasty morsels; just writing about them makes my mouth water.

A bowl with artichokes. Giovanna Garzoni (1600–1670)

Another way with these small artichokes is to give them a boil first, then bake them in little pies, with oysters and beef marrow, nicely seasoned with salt and pepper.*

We usually cook the larger ones on a grid over charcoal, having cut away the top halves of the leaves, and serve them with oil or melted butter, and salt and pepper. They taste even better if you squeeze some bitter orange juice over them after roasting; they appeal enormously to everyone who eats them like this.

We cook the very big artichokes, like those you have here, in water first; then we trim off the top halves of the biggest leaves and stuff between them oysters and some of their juices, morsels of beef marrow, oil or bits of fresh butter, and salt and pepper. Then we

*In very young, tender artichokes the chokes are not sufficiently developed to be inedible, so Castelvetro does not have to tell us to cut them away.

case them in pastry, and bake them, and they are delicious beyond belief.

A dish of broad beans.
Giovanna Garzoni
(1600–1670)

When artichokes start to get hard and woody, towards the end of the season, many growers cut off all the leaves and the choke and throw the hearts straight away into a bucket of water to keep them white. They sell these 'bottoms' as we call them, very cheaply – seven or eight for a Venetian *soldo*.

The best way of cooking these 'bottoms' is to stew them in a pot with oil, salt and pepper; or fry them in oil and serve them sprinkled with salt, pepper and bitter orange juice.

Artichoke hearts

These artichoke hearts can be preserved for winter use by boiling them a little in water, then draining them and putting them on a

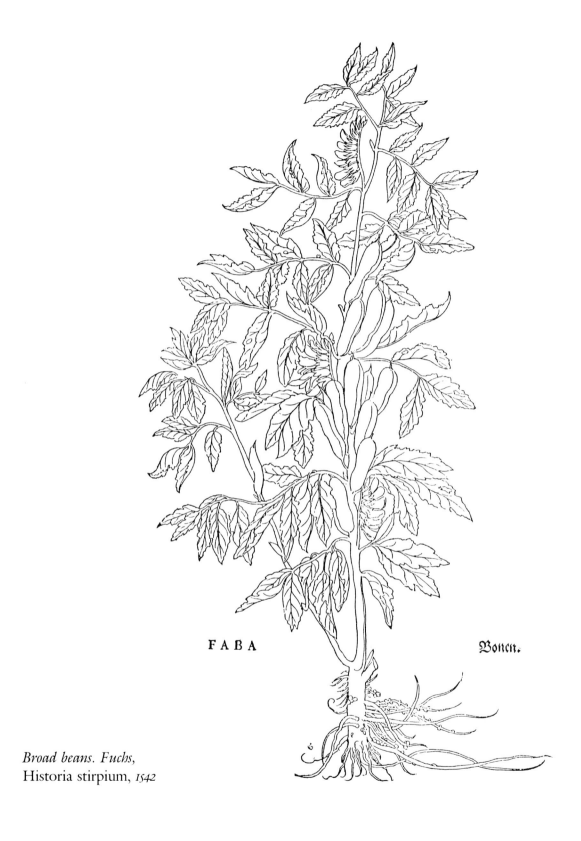

FABA   Bonen.

Broad beans. Fuchs,
Historia stirpium, *1542*

board to dry in the sun. When they are quite dry they should be stored well away from damp. Then when we come to eat them, they are reconstituted in tepid water, floured and fried, and seasoned with salt, pepper and bitter orange juice.

Fresh broad beans come next. We eat them at the end of a meal with a salty cheese from Crete or Sardinia, or failing that with Parmesan, and always with pepper. If there is no cheese, we just eat them with salt.

Broad beans

When broad beans start to become hard we cook them in water to loosen their skins, which we remove. Then we put the beans in a little pot with oil or fresh butter, and sweet herbs chopped very fine, and salt and pepper, and stew them gently, to make a really tasty little dish.

For the sake of brevity I will say no more about the many singular virtues of this vegetable, except to mention one. Broad bean flour is excellent for clearing impurities in the skin, and our ladies, who are delicate and fastidious in all their ways, use it in the bath instead of nitre, for its lather cleans them as well as anything else.

Before going any further I should say what I mean by 'sweet herbs' since I shall use this expression quite often. It is the name our housewives give to a special mixture of parsley, spinach beets, mint, borage, marjoram, basil and thyme (but with more of the first two since the others are so strongly flavoured), which they wash and then chop very fine. We use this mixture to season many dishes, especially fresh broad beans.

Sweet herbs

When they are hard and dry, as is particularly the case with field beans, we eat them in two different ways.

When cooked whole in salted water and eaten with oil and pepper they are called *fava de morti*, 'beans for the dead'. Beans cooked this way are seldom eaten by gentlefolk, except on the day that

Fava de morti – beans for the dead

superstitious papists dedicate to their dead, when custom has it that everyone prepares large quantities to give away to the poor, in the fond belief that this will relieve the excessive torments of their ancestors, languishing in purgatory.

Split beans   The second way, which is nicer and more usual, is to remove the outer skins and cook the beans in water and salt and season them with oil and pepper. They are sometimes cooked with sage leaves or rosemary and eaten as a lean dish in winter.

'Favetta'   Here is another recipe, which is somewhat more refined than the other two. Cook the beans in water with salt, and put them in a stone mortar with a little of their cooking liquid, and pound them with a wooden pestle until they are white as snow. Serve this *favetta* hot with olive oil, pepper and clean, washed raisins. Some use cinnamon as a seasoning instead of pepper.

Tortelli of favetta   Our ladies make *tortelli* with this purée, seasoned with pepper, which are really delicious. They take a sheet of very thin pastry, and cut out round shapes with a glass or a wooden cup, and put a spoonful of the purée on each one, adding a few raisins if desired. Then they fold each one up and make a neat little edging with their fingers and sprinkle them with flour. These *tortelli* will keep eight days or more.

When they come to cook them, they fry them in oil, and some send them to table sprinkled with honey or sugar. These crisp little morsels are so light they never fear for their precious teeth.

Peas   Next come peas. They are the noblest of vegetables, especially those whose pods are good to eat as well. They are cooked with herbs in both lean and fat dishes. For the latter we simmer them in good broth until half done, and then finish cooking them with a seasoning of hard bacon fat chopped with a knife or pounded in a mortar to the consistency of butter.

Peas. Mattioli, New Kreüterbuch, *1563*

For lean meals we cook our peas in a small amount of fresh salted water instead of broth, using oil to replace the bacon fat, and season them with strong spices and sweet herbs.

Mallow Mallow tips are good to eat when they are just on the point of flowering. We cut off about six or seven inches and strip away all the leaves, except for the one or two small, tender ones at the top, wrapped protectively round the little buds. They are cooked and eaten cold with oil, salt and pepper. Mallow eases constipation and gives considerable relief from painful urine.

Burdock Equally good are the white hearts, or rather shoots, of burdock, which spring up from the roots through the mass of leaves at the base of the plant. We peel off the bitter outer skin and, if we do not want to eat them straight away, throw the shoots into fresh water to keep them white. Eaten raw with salt and pepper they are as good as cardoons. They can be cooked in water, and eaten dressed with oil, salt and pepper.

Cardoons These should be sown now, so that they can be banked up in the autumn and enjoyed all through the winter, when artichokes are not in season. The cardoon is a kind of artichoke but it does not produce good heads. We eat the stems instead which, when banked up with earth, become white instead of green, crisp instead of woody, and sweet rather than bitter. Serve them raw, with pepper and salt, or cooked in good broth, as I explained in the recipe for tiny artichokes.

Salads And now the time has come for me to write about all the different kinds of salads we have at this time of year.

It is almost impossible to describe our delight in the delicious green salads of this joyful season. The cooked salads we ate in the winter seem so boring, while all this fresh greenery is a pleasure to the eye, a treat for the palate, and above all, a really important contribution to our health, purging us of all the unwholesome humours accumulated during the winter months.

The tender shoots of wild chicory are picked with a little of their roots. They are scraped, washed and served with oil, vinegar and salt in a bowl rubbed with garlic.

Wild chicory

Rampions are also good now. They are longish, crisp, little white roots, which also need to be scraped and can then be eaten raw in salads. They are greatly enjoyed by those who know about them. The leaves are edible as well.

Rampion

Some of my countrymen make a nice dish by cooking rampions in good meat broth and serving them with pepper and grated cheese on top.

Of all the salads we eat in the spring, the mixed salad is the best and most wonderful of all. Take young leaves of mint, those of garden cress, basil, lemon balm, the tips of salad burnet, tarragon, the flowers and tenderest leaves of borage, the flowers of swine cress, the young shoots of fennel, leaves of rocket, of sorrel, rosemary flowers, some sweet violets, and the tenderest leaves

An excellent mixed salad

I.
Cinera cum flore.

Thistle. Basilius Besler, Hortus Eystettensis, *1613*

or the hearts of lettuce. When these precious herbs have been picked clean and washed in several waters, and dried a little with a clean linen cloth, they are dressed as usual, with oil, salt and vinegar.

It takes more than good herbs to make a good salad, for success depends on how they are prepared. So, before going any further, I think I should explain exactly how to do this.

The right way to make a good salad

It is important to know how to wash your herbs, and then how to season them. Too many housewives and foreign cooks get their greenstuff all ready to wash and put it in a bucket of water, or some other pot, and slosh it about a little, and then, instead of taking it out with their hands, as they ought to do, they tip the leaves and water out together, so that all the sand and grit is poured out with them. Distinctly unpleasant to chew on . . .

So, you must first wash your hands, then put the leaves in a bowl of water, and stir them round and round, then lift them out carefully. Do this at least three or four times, until you can see that all the sand and rubbish has fallen to the bottom of the pot.

Next, you must dry the salad properly and season it correctly. Some cooks put their badly washed, barely shaken salad into a dish, with the leaves still so drenched with water that they will not take the oil, which they should to taste right. So I insist that first you must shake your salad really well and then dry it thoroughly with a clean linen cloth so that the oil will adhere properly. Then put it into a bowl in which you have previously put some salt and stir them together, and then add the oil with a generous hand, and stir the salad again with clean fingers or a knife and fork, which is more seemly, so that each leaf is properly coated with oil.

Never do as the Germans and other uncouth nations do – pile the badly washed leaves, neither shaken nor dried, up in a mound like a pyramid, then throw on a little salt, not much oil and far too much vinegar, without even stirring. And all this done to produce a decorative effect, where we Italians would much rather feast the palate than the eye.

You English are even worse; after washing the salad heaven knows how, you put the vinegar in the dish first, and enough of

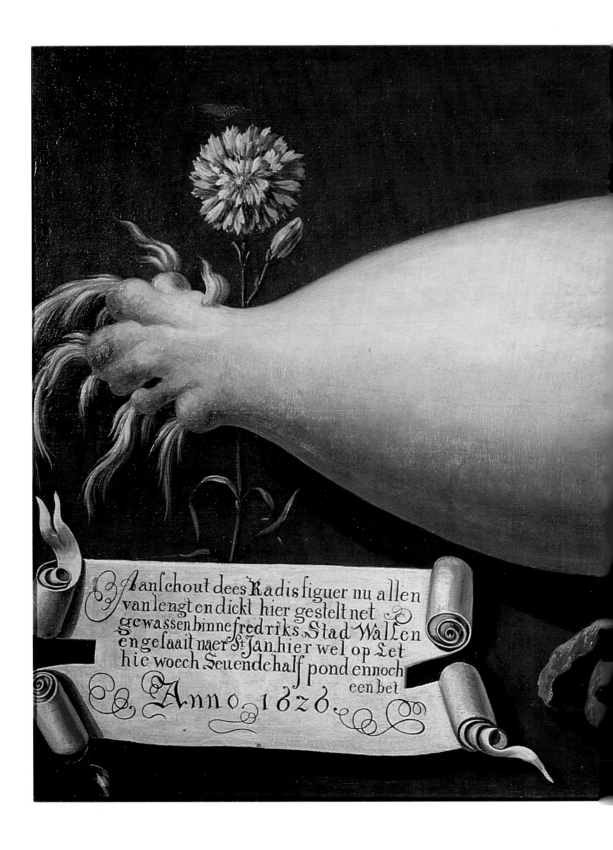

Aanschout dees Radis figuer nu allen
van lengt en dickt hier gestelt net
gewassen binne fredriks Stad Wallen
en gesaait naer St Jan hier wel op Let
hie woech Seuendehalf pond ennoch
een bet

Anno 1626

This monster radish, neatly washed, weighed 7½lb 'and a bit more'.
It was grown in Fredriks Stad in 1626

that for a footbath for Morgante, and serve it up, unstirred, with neither oil nor salt, which you are supposed to add at table. By this time some of the leaves are so saturated with vinegar that they cannot take the oil, while the rest are quite naked and fit only for chicken food.

So, to make a good salad the proper way, you should put the oil in first of all, stir it into the salad, then add the vinegar and stir again. And if you do not enjoy this, complain to me.

The secret of a good salad is plenty of salt, generous oil and little vinegar, hence the text of the Sacred Law of Salads:

> *Insalata ben salata,*
> *poco aceto e ben oliata.*

> Salt the salad quite a lot,
> then generous oil put in the pot,
> and vinegar, but just a jot.

And whosoever transgresses this benign commandment is condemned never to enjoy a decent salad in their life, a fate which I fear lies in store for most of the inhabitants of this kingdom.

Olla podrida   In Italy we make another salad with the outlandish name of *olla podrida* because as well as the profusion of salad ingredients I have just described, we go on to add white endive, blanched chicory shoots, the cooked roots of these two vegetables, raisins, angelica, stoned olives, salted capers soaked in tepid water, some little Genoese capers, thin slices of salted ox tongue, small pieces of candied citron and lemon peel, spring onions if they are in season, radishes, horseradish, and the white shoots of alexanders.

Alexanders   Cooked or raw, these shoots make a nice salad on their own. In spring the roots are good, too. We eat them cooked, on their own, or with other vegetables.

There is little left to say about spring salads, except to mention that in France I once learned how to make one out of nothing but

The hunt picnic. Carlo Cane (1618–88)

cabbage, finely sliced, which was really very good. Since then I often do this when there is nothing else to be had for a salad, and it is always acceptable.

Mulberries

Now I come to that really useful tree, the mulberry, which we treasure both for its leaves, on which the noble silkworm feeds, and its delicious fruit, which when in season nourishes the chickens in the barnyard.

There are two kinds of mulberry tree. One grows tall and broad and has small, tender, greenish-yellow leaves. Its fruit is white and very sweet, though not much esteemed (except by silly women and small children), but is excellent for rearing little chickens and

Female emperor moth and wild strawberries.
Jacques le Moyne de Morgues (1530–88)

other fowl, who love it, and fatten quite well on it.

The other mulberry does not grow to the same size. Its leaves are bigger and its fruits are larger and black when ripe, with a sour-sweet flavour which is most agreeable and wholesome. We also serve them for dessert in the form of mulberry paste.

Strawberries

In Italy, it is only in spring that we have these fragrant and health-giving berries, whereas you happy mortals, though you do not get them so early, have them twice a year, in mid June and in October. Last year I was in Cambridge on 28 October, and was amazed to be eating strawberries by the plateful, not just one or two. They were exquisite.

Strawberries are one of the healthiest fruits to eat and would not even harm an invalid. A decoction made from both leaves and roots is good to drink for inflammation of the liver and regulates the kidneys and the bladder. Used as a mouthwash it hardens the gums, strengthens the teeth and clears catarrh.

Gooseberries

Next we have gooseberries, which we vastly prefer to eat sour rather than ripe. Quite the reverse of you English, who are so fond of sweet dishes (although I notice that in recent years your nobility has taken to putting gooseberries in the sauce they serve with goose).

Your taste for sweet food is probably due to the fact that you never have to endure, as we do in Italy, the loss of appetite caused by the intense summer heat. We like to revive our jaded palates with sharp things, and so we put sour gooseberries in sauces for chicken, squabs and boiled veal. When gooseberries are not in season we use verjuice, the juice of unripe grapes.

We also make excellent tarts with gooseberries, while you in this country make them into very good pies, with sugar and cinnamon.

Elder flowers

Towards the end of spring, the elder comes into bloom, and makes wonderful fritters. Mix the blossoms with *ricotta*, Parmesan, egg,

*Still life with
elderflowers. Anon.
Florentine,
seventeenth century*

and powdered cinnamon, and shape the mixture into little crescent shapes. Flour them lightly and fry them in butter, and send to table sprinkled with sugar.

If you put some of the dried flowers into vinegar and leave the bottle for a while in the sun, it makes the vinegar much stronger and gives it a delightful flavour.

A pinch of dried elder flowers, tied up in a piece of clean linen and left in a barrel of good sweet white wine, will give it a muscat flavour. In Italy many of our innkeepers do rather well out of this, passing the wine off as genuine muscat wine, and making quite a profit for themselves.

Gooseberries, redcurrants and cherries.
Johann Walther, c. 1652

Aubergines At the end of this lovely season, aubergines start to be good. Beautiful to look at, they are more or less the size of apples, but oval, with a shiny skin like a gourd. Some are all white, some white mottled with pink, and some violet. A little bush no more than a yard high will produce fifteen to twenty aubergines.

One way of preparing aubergines is to cut them open down the middle, hollow them out and fill them with a mixture of the chopped pulp, breadcrumbs, egg, grated cheese, sweet herbs and butter or oil, and bitter orange juice. Then either grill them over charcoal, or stew them gently in an earthenware pot or tinned copper dish.

Another way is to slice them and fry them in oil, and eat them sprinkled with salt and pepper and bitter orange juice.

Because they are hot and wet, they help to induce sleep, but it is unhealthy to eat too many of them.

Melanzana¹fructupallido.

Aubergine. Basilius Besler, Hortus Eystettensis, *1613*

Flowers and fruit (detail). Paolo Porpora (1617–73)

Summer

In this, the hottest of the seasons, we use far more fresh fruit and vegetables, and dishes made from them, than meat, which in the extreme heat seems quite nauseating. Of all nations in the world, we take pride of place in our profusion of good, refreshing fruit in summertime. But I must keep to my plan and start by describing the salads and then go on to fruit.

Hearted lettuce

Most of the salads we eat in the summer are made from lettuce. The crisp, white, *capucina* is refreshing and at the same time induces the sweet sleep that the heat disturbs and dispels.

We also eat this lettuce cooked. Cut the solid heart into four parts, each well oiled and salted and peppered, and roast them on a grid over hot charcoal (not burning embers) and eat them sprinkled with orange juice. They are delicious, almost as good as asparagus.

These lettuce hearts are also good stewed or braised.

Cos lettuce

As well as the *capucina* lettuce, there is the *romana*, with its much longer, smooth leaves, which our ingenious gardeners tie tightly together round a cane, so that the insides blanch as white as snow and become wonderfully crisp.

Purslane

Purslane is eaten a lot as a salad on its own, or with other herbs; we always add pepper and finely chopped onion to counteract its coldness.

Cucumbers At the same time cucumbers are good. Because of their coldness, they are served with onions and pepper, or stewed with gooseberries or verjuice. We never use the large yellow ones in salads, as the English do, but only the small, completely green cucumbers.

We make another dish with the big ones, which is very good. Cut them in half lengthways and hollow out the soft part inside. Then fill them with a stuffing of finely chopped herbs, breadcrumbs, an egg, grated cheese and oil or butter, all mixed together. Roast them on a grid, or cook them gently in an earthenware pot or a tinned copper dish with a lid. You could add pepper or spices.

Sweet fennel At about the same time young, sweet fennel bulbs appear, which we eat raw with salt after meals.

The young shoots make an excellent Lenten dish, cooked in water and eaten with oil, salt and pepper. This tastes delicious and is incredibly healthy as well.

This herb has two good effects. One is that it improves the taste of bad wine. Our villainous Venetian wine-sellers solicitously offer innocent or simple-minded customers a piece of nice fennel to eat with their wine, or a few nuts, insisting that otherwise they might do themselves harm by drinking wine on an empty stomach . . .

The other virtue of fennel is that it warms a cold stomach, gets rid of wind, aids digestion and sweetens bad breath.

We preserve quantities of fresh fennel in good white wine vinegar and eat it in summer and in winter when offering drinks to friends between meals. We also serve this pickle with fruit on special occasions, when fresh fennel is not to be had.

Fennel seeds are gathered in the autumn. We flavour various dishes with them, and eat them on their own after meals.

How to grow sweet fennel I would like to explain here how sweet fennel can be grown from
from bitter seeds the bitter kind. Some people do this by planting the bitter seeds inside a dried fig, others sow them in old pig manure.

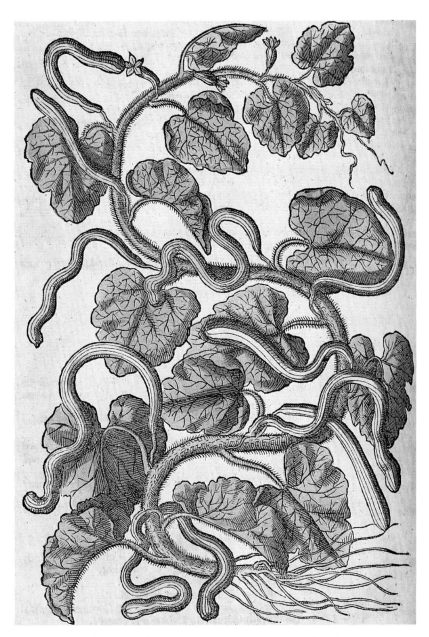

Snake cucumbers. Mattioli, New Kreüterbuch, *1563*

Allegory of summer. Lucas van Valkenborch (1535–97)

Early figs   Towards the end of May the 'flower figs' are good. These early, or first-crop, figs are so called because this noble tree produces, instead of flowers, a fruit even bigger than the real fruit which it bears in early September, and which I shall describe later on. In Venice they call this the Madonna fig, for no good reason that I can think of.

Lupins   Our womenfolk and little children nibble at lupin beans between meals during the hottest summer days. They are very bitter but can easily be sweetened by putting them in a canal or deep stream of clear, running water, in a tightly fastened bag secured to a pole or hook, so that the current flows right through them. The lupins are left there for two or three whole days, until they have lost their bitterness and become sweet. Then they are peeled and salted and nibbled more as a snack than anything else, the sort of thing that

Chinese bowl with figs.
Giovanna Garzoni
(1600–1670)

only appeals to pregnant women or silly children. Dried lupins are used to fatten pigs and other animals.

Although this is somewhat outside my main theme, I must mention the fact that, wherever lupins are grown, they drive away moles, who flee their accustomed nests and go looking for lodgings elsewhere. Indeed, to clear a whole field of them you only have to plant twenty of the seeds in different places.

How to rid fields of troublesome moles

Mole and mouse. Jacopo Ligozzi (1547–1627)

The foliage of lupins has the peculiar quality of enriching poor soil, however sterile it may be. So good farmers sow them on their least fertile land, and when the lupins are just about to produce pods, they plough them in, which soon transforms the barren fields into productive ones, quite cheaply, to the farmers' considerable advantage.

A cheap way to enrich poor soil

Early in the summer come muscat pears, which also grow in England, but do not ripen so early. Although they are a small fruit, everyone likes them because of their musky scent, hence the names *muscardini, muscatelli*.

Muscat pears

In midsummer there are *armelini*, a variety which ripens earlier than apricots. They are smaller and not so well-flavoured. Apri-

Apricots

cots are ready a little later, although considerably earlier than they are here. Both have very sweet kernels from which our druggists make excellent confections. With us the season lasts three weeks or a bit more. Apricots are usually eaten raw, but they make delicious and healthy sweetmeats when crystallized or preserved in syrup.

Luglienga grapes

At the beginning of July the *luglienga* grapes, named after the month, are ready to eat. Although not the best in the world, they are somewhat over-esteemed for being the first to ripen. These grapes are quite harmless, unlike some others. Since they are rather weak, we do not make much wine out of them; in fact most of them get eaten anyway.

Muscat grapes

These are followed by muscat grapes, which are much better. An excellent heavy wine is made from them, to which they give its name, *muscatello* or *muscato*. We make very little of it around Modena, my native city, but much more in other parts of Italy.

Tremarina grapes

These two are followed by the *tremarina* grape, which I imagine must get its name from the way in which it hangs tremulously from its beloved mother-plant, quivering in every whispering breeze.

This vine produces grapes as tiny as peas, with just two or three bigger ones in each bunch. They are without doubt the same dried grapes which are imported into England from the island of Zakinthos, which you call Corinth raisins. These are used all over the world, but nowhere consumed in such unbelievably enormous quantities as in this country, where you put them into all kinds of dishes, especially your Christmas puddings.

Raisins are also used a lot in various medicaments. I can recall to this day an occasion when one in particular was such a help to me, and I would be failing in my duty to my fellow men if I omitted to pass on this sovereign remedy.

I was once living in the neighbourhood of San Grigioni, in the small but pleasant village of Piuri, a mile and a half from the rather larger town of Chiavenna, when I was taken ill with a serious and dangerous affliction, an unbelievably unpleasant attack of constipation. It was so bad that I went for ten or eleven days without relief, which when it came caused such intense pain that I do not believe a woman in childbirth could have suffered more than I. In this sorry state, hoping that God in His mercy might cure me, I took myself off on some errand or other to Chiavenna. When I got there I went straight to the pharmacy of Francesco Bottighisio of Bergamo. (This distinguished man was obliged to live in exile there because of his religious views.)

A great virtue of this grape

He greeted me affectionately and asked me kindly how I came to be so yellow and bloated, and when he heard about my affliction, smiled and said: 'There's no question but that with God's help I

85

The dispensary.
Paolo Antonio
Barbieri

shall soon be able to clear this up for you; come back tomorrow for something I shall have got ready for you.' So I thanked him and went back to Piuri, and returned the next day to find that he had prepared a medicine for me in the following way: Take one ounce of raisins and soak them in dry, not sweet, malmsey. Drain them in a sieve, and when they have dried a little, mix them with a dram of powdered rhubarb.

I was to take some of these raisins when I got up in the morning and walk up and down the room chewing them, before swallowing them. This I did straight away, and after only two doses, I was completely cured of my unpleasant affliction. Ever since then, and that was over forty years ago, I have never been constipated for more than two or three days without relief.

That is all I have to say about this remedy, except that the dose is a spoonful, and that if I don't have any malmsey, I use a good white wine instead. I have, to my credit, used this medicine to help many a sufferer.

Some very good pears now come into season. The *ghiacciuoli* is one which I do not recall ever seeing in England. It is somewhat bigger than the muscat pear and highly thought of.

Ghiacciuoli pears

Early in August we enjoy *gnocchi* or *sozzobuoni* pears. They are about the same size as the ones you call Catherine pears, and I have never seen them, let alone eaten them, outside Italy. They fill the mouth with an unbelievably delicious juice, which tastes rather like melons.

Gnocchi pears

When unripe they are green in colour, but are hardly ever left to ripen on the tree. We pick them about 20 July, while they are still immature, and leave them to ripen in fresh straw for ten or fifteen days, until they become perfectly ripe and soft, but yellowish and not very pretty to look at.

They are grown in such huge quantities round Bologna and Modena that they can be sent by the bargeload as far as Venice, and still sold cheaply, even there, which you won't find happening in many parts of Italy.

Grapes and pears.
Giovanna Garzoni
(1600–1670)

Melons As June comes to an end the melons start to be good. I take my hat off to this fruit; it is my favourite for no other reason than its marvellous sweet scent, the most wonderful perfume in the world. Believe me, none of the foreign melons have the fragrance that ours have, not even those of Provence or Spain, for all the care and trouble they take to produce even just a few fairly good varieties.

A wonderful characteristic of the melon Melons are marvellously refreshing to the system. They are excellent for those who are troubled with kidney stones and will cure burning urine between midday and starlight.

Zatte and other melons Melons continue until September. The traveller in Italy will get best value buying *poppone* and *gavagnini* in Venice, *liliotti* in Bologna, *scotie* and *muscatelli* in Modena and *romanette* in Genoa. The *zatte*, which are yet another kind, go on rather longer. They are at their best and most plentiful around Padua.

Melon peel makes a nice stew. It is given to thoroughbred horses as a tonic or purgative.

The secret of how to preserve melons Melons can be preserved for a long time, by taking them from their mother plants while still young and putting them in a jar of honey. This was discovered by chance in the city of Modena, where by God's grace I was born. A prosperous grocer had his shop next to the part of the market-place where these fruit were sold, and it often happened that gentlemen who liked to select melons for themselves, would find that their servants were not at hand to carry them home, and would leave the bags in the grocer's shop, sometimes until lunch-time, when they would remember to send for them.

One day a large number of melons were deposited there, and the apprentices piled them all up on a bench, over some pots of honey. The bench collapsed under the weight, and one of the melons fell unobserved into one of the honey pots. They searched for it in vain, but it did not turn up until the grocer came to empty the pot some considerable time later and discovered the missing melon, much to his surprise, and the delight of his apprentices, who of course had been accused of eating it. So they took the

88

melon out, and wiped it clean and restored it to its owner as fresh and good as the day it was first picked. He cut it open and found it unexpectedly good. Everyone was delighted, not just at the recovery of the fruit, but by this happy discovery, which has been so useful to so many ever since.

Market scene. Joachim Beuckelaer (c. 1530/35–73/4)

In fact one shouldn't be surprised at this, for it is only one of the many exceptional qualities of honey, the most amazing perhaps being its capacity, which I know from my own experience, to preserve grafts or scions, especially those from wild fruit trees. This is how it is done:

Have ready a container of tin filled with honey and place it under the tree from which you intend to take the scions; these should be

How to preserve grafts

Melons. Giovanna Garzoni (1600–1670)

put into the tin as soon as they are taken. Then you must close it carefully and seal it with soft wax, and cover the tin tightly with waxed silk.

This is what I did a good twenty years ago, when I happened to be in Copenhagen, the capital city of Denmark. After tasting a most delicate pear, which pleased me enormously, in a fine orchard there, I marked the tree on which it grew and took some scions. Several months later, I found myself in the service of Duke Charles of Sweden, who, as I predicted, was later to be elected king by popular acclaim. He took an interest in many ingenious and worthwhile activities, especially the ancient and (whatever the low and ignorant may say) noble art of agriculture. He was particularly skilful at grafting, so I offered him the ones I had taken six months earlier, which were still perfectly preserved.

When spring came he was at his estate in the small port of Nyköping. He sent for me one day and together, in his charming orchard, we grafted the scions on to several of the trees, where, to his great delight, they flourished!

Watermelons But now I must pick up my thread again, by going on to say that early in July we have watermelons, which some claim to be another kind of cucumber. They are extremely thirst-quenching, being little more than a pleasant, sweet-tasting juice which fills the mouth and is marvellously refreshing. The fruit is round rather

than long, and its skin is green and smooth like a gourd. The best watermelons are red inside, others are yellow, and the least good are white. Their seeds are bigger and harder than melon seeds, with a black or brown shell, and are very good to eat as they are, or in confectionery.

Watermelon.
Mattioli,
New Kreüterbuch, *1563*

Hazelnuts   The best of the green hazelnuts come about the middle of August. They are longish, with a sort of red fuzz on the kernels, or 'grains' as we call them. They are very good coated with sugar; indeed for some years now our confectioners have been using them instead of almonds.

There are other hazelnuts, bigger and rounder, which are ready as early as the feast of St Peter [29 June], but are not so well thought of as the later ones.

Hazelnuts are good to eat both green and dried. We keep the dried ones for eating in winter and during Lent. Some people think they are indigestible, and bad for the catarrh, but then, as the proverb says:

Ogni cosa è sana al huomo sano.

Everything is wholesome to the healthy.

Almonds   Green almonds are good about now, or even earlier, but are not in season long; they are much healthier than hazelnuts, and considered to be the noblest nut of all. Many people in Italy, especially in Tuscany, eat them green when the shell is still soft, or cook them like truffles.

Almond paste is made into all kinds of delicious and wholesome confections, as well as marzipan, most of which are quite common here. Not so well known, however, are almond and bread soup, almond milk and almond butter.

Walnuts   We also have walnuts, which are common everywhere. The green ones start to be good about the feast of St Lawrence [10 August], and are highly esteemed and eaten by the gentry, who consider the dried ones to be rather coarse and unrefined.

Agliata   Dried walnuts are used in a garlic sauce called *agliata*, and this is how you make it: first take the best and whitest walnut kernels, in the quantity you need, and pound them in a really clean stone mortar (not a metal one) in which you have first crushed two or three cloves of garlic. When they are all well mixed, take three slices of stale white bread, well soaked in a good meat broth which

is not too fatty, and pound them with the nuts. When everything is well mixed, thin the sauce out with some of the same warm meat broth, until you have a liquid like the pap they give to little babies. Serve it tepid, with a little crushed pepper.

Prudent folk eat this sauce with fresh pork as an antidote to its harmful qualities, or with boiled goose, an equally indigestible food. Serious pasta eaters even enjoy *agliata* with macaroni and lasagne. It is also good with boletus mushrooms, which I shall describe in due course.

In Lombardy they make oil from the poorer quality nuts, which they use to light the stables. Poor people and even worthy artisans use it in lamps about the house or on the table. The peasants in the countryside use nothing else for their lamps. This oil is good for various ailments. It also makes furniture made out of walnut wood – bedsteads, tables, benches and so forth – shine like a mirror.

Still life with fruit.
Cornelis de Heem
(1631–95)

Walnut oil

Overleaf:
Fruit stall. Anon.
North Italian, 1601

93

Marrows (zucchini) Right at the end of this scorching season come long, white marrows about as thick as an arm, though not all of them reach that size.

Peel the small, tender ones, cut them in slices, not too thick, and flour them and fry them in oil. Serve them sprinkled with salt and pepper, and *agresto* or lemon juice, which is not a bad alternative.

The larger *zucchini* make a nice stew. Boil them in salted water, and when they are almost done add a decent amount of sweet herbs, finely chopped spring onions, olive oil and at least a ladleful of unripe grapes or *agresto*.

Our confectioners preserve quantities of the biggest and plumpest of these marrows in sugar; we call them *zuccato*, and use them in various fine dishes.

Beans I have already dealt with broad beans, from garden and field, in the section on spring, and now I want to describe two other kinds of bean which taste rather like them, although neither is eaten raw. The least well known and the largest, we call 'Turkish' [exotic] beans; they are white or flecked with pink and tan. The other kind of bean is smaller, white or faintly pinkish with a black spot in the middle.

To take the first kind, they grow very tall, so you should either grow them against a trellis, or, if you want a good crop, plant them out when they are a foot high and train them up rows of dried twigs or branches. These beans have such lovely green foliage that our Italian ladies, especially the Venetians, who are so fond of shade and greenery, and fonder still of peering out at passers-by without being seen, grow them in large wooden boxes on their windowsills. These boxes are as wide as the windows, about a foot high, and the same depth. They fill them with good soil, and plant ten or twelve beans at full moon in February, March or April. Then they train them up elegant white trellises to screen the whole window with a pleasant shade.

Our gardeners, too, make neat rows of white cannabis stalks in

their plots, and train these beans up them, which is a lovely sight and produces an abundant crop.

The bean-eater.
Annibale Carracci
(1560–1609)

The pods of these Turkish beans, when they are young and tender, and not fully mature, make an excellent salad, boiled, and eaten cold with olive oil and bitter orange juice.

When they are bigger, they are very good boiled, and served cut up in small pieces in a dish with butter and salt and pepper.

The dried beans, shelled, and cooked in broth, make a tasty stew.

The other kind of bean, which we call native or domestic, are sown in large quantities in the wheat-fields after the harvest. They do

Dwarf beans

not grow high, so have to be kept really free from weeds, and need to be hoed quite often, especially after rain.

We eat the cooked tender green pods as a salad, and do the same with the shelled fresh beans.

Dried, they make a dish for lean days, especially at harvest time, when the peasants coming in from the fields consider themselves well-treated when we welcome them with a bowlful of these beans served with some of the cheese and butter left over from the market.

This is how we cook them: sort out the bad or damaged beans, wash them in tepid water to remove any earth, and simmer them in plain water in a clean pot until they are half-done. Then strain them and continue cooking them in a fresh lot of water and salt, not forgetting plenty of oil, and pepper, their best seasoning. Beans cooked this way are really delicious. Some add shelled and peeled dried chestnuts, which go rather well with the beans.

Tarts and fritters   We pound cooked, unseasoned beans in a mortar, put the mixture through a sieve and add honey and strong spices, and then use this

Basket of fruit. Michelangelo Merisi da Caravaggio (1573–1610)

*Paduan
countrywoman.
Late sixteenth
century*

as a filling for little tarts or pies, made with sheets of very thin pastry mixed with lard instead of the usual butter. We cook these in the oven, or over the fire on large trays of tinned copper under an earthenware lid. Alternatively, these little pastries can be fried in lard and eaten just as they are, or with a little honey.

When you consider the reasons, it is hardly surprising that we Italians eat such a profusion of fruit and vegetables, some of them quite unknown and unappreciated elsewhere. Firstly, Italy, though beautiful, is not as plentifully endowed as France or this fertile island with meat, so we make it our business to devise other ways of feeding our excessive population.

The other equally powerful reason is that the heat, which persists for almost nine months of the year, has the effect of making meat seem quite repellent, especially beef, which in such a temperature one can hardly bear to look at, let alone eat. Even mutton is not eaten much, for we keep the animals closed in stalls at night, not in the fields as you do, and this gives the meat a somewhat unpleasant taste.

*Why Italians eat more
fruit and vegetables
than meat*

*Overleaf:
The old man of Artimino.
Giovanna Garzoni
(1600–1670)*

This is why we prefer our fruit and vegetables, for they are refreshing, they do not thicken the blood and above all they revive the flagging appetite.

Chickpeas But let me get back to the point – the other vegetables we enjoy at this time of year. White and red chickpeas, the latter being the most wholesome, are some of the healthiest vegetables you can find.

Take a ladleful of the red chickpeas and boil them in unsalted water with plenty of oil, and when they are cooked squeeze lemon juice over them. The liquid from this is taken by sufferers from kidney stones, or other kidney complaints, to alleviate pain in urinating. If lemon juice is not available, radish juice has more or less the same effect.

The length of time chickpeas take to cook depends on the quality of the soil they were grown in. When you have some of the kind which take a long time to cook, leave them to soak all night long in a pot with some hot charcoal tied in a piece of coarse, clean linen. Next morning rinse the chickpeas well in tepid water and put them in a pan or earthenware pot with fresh water and salt. If the water is not going to be drunk as a medicament, add some sage and rosemary, a moderate amount of oil, and, for those who like it, two or three cloves of garlic.

On summer evenings after supper, our good ladies sit around in droves on their doorsteps, and when they see the countrywomen coming home from the fields with baskets full of tender young chickpeas, they buy quantities of them just for fun, to nibble at raw.

Lentils Like many other countries we also have lentils, one of the most, if not the most, unhealthy vegetables one can eat, except for the broth, which, they say, is a miraculous drink for children with smallpox. In general lentils are only eaten by the lowest of the low.

Next we have another vegetable called vetch, which tastes rather like chickpeas. We cook them the way we do beans, but they are considered a rather common food, for they generate wind, bad blood and considerable melancholy.

Grass pea

Then we have rice, which is eaten in many countries, but grown in few. We plant it in low-lying places, under water. It has a good yield, and is a most useful crop. It is a good food for the able-bodied, but hard to digest. The Turks eat more rice than any other nation, and cook it in many different and delicate ways.

Rice

In Italy we have more millet than in England. It is a kind of grain used for bread in times of scarcity. It will keep a good ten years or more, and the Venetian government, for this reason, stores large supplies of millet in its fortresses.

Common millet

The grain is small and straw-coloured. It is excellent for feeding fowl and fattening chickens, pigeons and, above all, quails, turtle-doves and geese, who become unbelievably fat. I swear I have seen some in Venice, fed on a mash made from millet, that weighed forty or fifty pounds or more, whose livers were as big as calves' livers and pale as snow.

The Jews fatten up enormous quantities of geese, since they eat them instead of pork, which is forbidden them in the Laws of Moses, and they never sell one for less than 15 guineas each.

Bread made from millet is good on the first day, but not so good on the next. This bread is also good for thickening stews.

Common Millet. Jacques le Moyne de Morgues (1530–88)

This is a grain very like the preceding one. It is used in soups and stews, but is not very nutritious. It helps to cure dysentery, as do rice and millet. Applied externally, a poultice of foxtail millet is drying and soothing. Millet is sometimes used in pies.

Foxtail millet

And that is all I can recall of the fruit and vegetables of this, the hottest season. So I now go on to describe those of the temperate autumn.

Fruit and vegetables with parrot. Johann Walther, c. *1652*

Autumn

Autumn in Italy is so temperate and delightful, with such an abundance of every kind of fruit, that we have the saying:

L'autunno per la bocca et la primavera per l'occhio.

Spring is for looking, autumn for tasting.

And indeed in my province, *la grassa Lombardia,** if a nobleman has to send someone from his household on a long journey he will give him very little money for his expenses, knowing very well that for the entire length of the journey he will be able to have as much fruit as he wants, without spending a penny.

Salads

First I shall deal with the salads of this season, which are more or less the same as the ones we eat in the spring. But as well as mixed salads and lettuce, the crisp, white endive starts to appear, and lasts all through the winter.

Chicory

When endive is not available we use the tender, green leaves and shoots of chicory, which we chop up fine and serve in a dish rubbed with garlic, and the usual condiments.

Cauliflowers

For beauty and goodness these take pride of place in the cabbage family. First cooked in salted water, cauliflowers are served cold, dressed with olive oil, salt and pepper. They also make an excellent dish, cooked in broth and served on slices of bread, with some of the broth poured over, and seasoned with grated mature cheese and pepper.

*The district round Padua, not Lombardy as we know it today.

Hearted cabbage

These start at the beginning of autumn and go on through most of the winter. They are cooked in various ways, besides the English manner, which I quite like.

Slice a cabbage finely and cook it in a pot in good broth. When it is half done add a mixture of parsley, beets, borage, thyme and hard bacon fat, chopped with a knife until the fat is creamed, and continue cooking the cabbage on a low heat. Serve it with grated cheese and pepper. You can add two or three cloves of garlic to the fat and herb mixture, which makes it much tastier if you don't mind the smell of this health-giving plant.

Another way is to take a whole cabbage and simmer it in broth until it is half cooked. Then hollow out the middle and stuff it with some of the cabbage you have removed, chopped and mixed with herbs, bacon, breadcrumbs, grated cheese, pepper and one or two eggs. Finish cooking the stuffed cabbage in a fresh pan of broth on a low heat and serve it whole. Strong spices, pepper and a little garlic make a good addition to the stuffing.

Sometimes we boil the cabbage whole in salted water and then cut it into four or more pieces and cover them with melted butter, season them with salt and pepper, and leave them to mature in a covered dish on the fire until it is time to serve them up. This method is not at all bad.

By the end of the season all the other kinds of cabbage are good, because they will have had their first touch of frost. The more frost they get, the better they are.

Savoy cabbage

These are green on the outside and white in the middle, but crisp and open, not closed like the hearted cabbage. Some are curly and some are not; the curly ones are the best.

One way of cooking these cabbages is to simmer them in rich broth with a piece of salt pork.

Another way makes a dish for lean days – cook the cabbage in salted water and when nearly done add a generous ladle of oil and at least two or three cloves of garlic, which this dish really needs, and season it with pepper.

Vegetable and fruit stall.
Pieter Aertsen
1508/9–75)

If you have no salt pork for the first recipe, you can use some yellow sausage or a *mortadella*, which you must first wash well in hot water. I can assure you that these taste even better.

Note that if the stalk is left in the ground all winter, after the cabbage has been cut off, little shoots will grow on it in the spring. I described these in the section on spring vegetables.

Cabbage stalks, dried in the sun or in the oven, can be ground to a powder, and make a tried and trusted remedy for pains in the chest. The weight of a gold *scudo* of this powder, taken in good beef or chicken broth, not too fat or too salty, will loosen the chest, and so save the life, of sufferers from the stitch or *point de côté*, as the French call it.

Green cabbage There is another kind of cabbage which we only eat as a cooked salad, dressed with oil and vinegar. It is all green and grows no higher than a foot or thereabouts, and forms a big head, like broccoli, and should be treated in the same way – not overcooked, and well seasoned. To do this we bring a pot of water to a rolling boil and plunge the well-washed cabbage into it two or three times, holding it by the stem. When seasoned as I have described above, it is as good as broccoli.

White cabbage There are also white cabbages, which, like the preceding one, are not yet known in England. This excellent cabbage has a very big head, about the size of a hearted cabbage, with very thick stalks. It is cooked in rich meat broth.

Kohlrabi Then we have kohlrabi. The leaves are quite nice, but the so-called root, really the base of the stem, is absolutely delicious. It makes a marvellous dish cooked in rich broth and dished up with grated cheese, salt, pepper and spices.

Peaches About the middle of August or later peaches begin to be ripe. They last all September and part of October.

This delicate fruit is usually eaten raw. Some eat peaches unpeeled, after wiping the skin with a clean cloth, and quote in justification the saying:

Peaches.
Giovanna Garzoni
(1600–1670)

> *A l'amico monda il fico,*
> *e il persico al nemico.*
>
> Peel a fig for a friend,
> and a peach for an enemy.

This may also be taken to mean that peaches are as unwholesome as they are delicious. For this reason they are steeped in good wine, which is supposed to draw out the harmful qualities. I very much doubt that these exist; I am sure that it is gluttony rather than hygiene that accounts for this practice. Peaches certainly taste much better with wine, and I notice that nobody ever throws away the wine that they have soaked in, or comes to any harm from drinking it.

Some people eat peaches cooked, wrapped in damp paper and roasted in the ashes – these really are very nice.

They are very good preserved whole in sugar or made into a stiff paste called *persicata*. Our ladies also dry large quantities of them, cut in half with the stones removed, for eating in Lent.

Peach stones are used medicinally. The shell and kernel, when powdered with other ingredients, will dissolve kidney stones so that they can be passed through the bladder. The bitter kernel is used in remedies for internal obstructions, and also for worms in small children.

Figs

I must not forget to mention figs, which we have in vast quantities, and which everyone eats raw. We do not have many dried figs in my part of Italy, though they are common in other regions, and are very good indeed, particularly with almonds. Confectioners preserve them whole with peeled almonds in the shape of Dutch cheeses, a delicious sweetmeat, which they keep to eat during Lent.

Dried figs, roasted a little and eaten at bedtime, will help to clear up those nasty coughs that linger after a bad cold. But make sure the figs are not stale.

Apples & pears

Here should have been the place to describe the enormous quantity of apples and pears that we have in such profusion, but since to do so would take up more space than I have room for, I shall limit myself to describing only those varieties which you do not have in England.

Paradise apple

One of these we call the paradise apple; it is about the same size as the one you have here called the 'two-year apple', but its skin is yellow and speckled with little blood-red spots. The longer it is kept, the better it becomes. These apples not only taste delicious, but have a wonderful sweet smell, and will scent linen sheets if laid

*Still life with
Christ at Emmaus.
Attributed to
Floris van Dijk*

between them. The peel, thrown on a shovel of coals, will fill a room with the aroma. It is also used to perfume ointments.

Bergamot pear   I do not recall ever having seen the bergamot pear in England. It is shaped more like an apple than a pear, and is green in colour, turning yellow as it ripens, when it is full of a delicate juice quite unlike anything else. Its only fault is that it does not keep well.

Garzegnuolo pear   This is rather like your warden pear, which we do not have; it is a fine and noble fruit, and compares very well with it, as those numerous gentlemen who have been to Italy will testify.

The common grape   And now we come to grapes, a splendid fruit, of which we must have more than most countries, both for eating and wine-making. The number of varieties is enormous. As well as the ones I described earlier, we have *Trebbiano, Albana, Tosca, Marzemino,* all of which make copious amounts of the most delicate wine. Then we have *Rosetta, Pignuola,* and a profusion of others which make wines of so many different flavours and qualities that we are the wonder of the world. We have such a superabundance of grapes that I often wonder how it can be worthwhile for people to bother to make wine, and all the other products of the vine, when they can buy them so cheaply. We seem, however, to be in the habit of doing so. I've often heard it said that a moderate drinker can buy himself a year's supply of wine for as little as four *scudi*. It would be hard to get as much beer for so little in England.

Grapes are devoured in large quantities by birds and beasts, including cows, sheep, pigs, dogs, foxes, wolves and chickens. Humans eat a great many too, both fresh and dried.

Agresto   The amounts used to make *agresto* are unbelievable, because this requires unripe grapes, which have less juice in them. Every family with an acre of land makes at least a barrel of it. *Sapa* (which we also call *vin cotto*), and grape sauce, are also made in huge quantities, as well as *mostarda*.

114

Varieties of grapes (detail). Bartolomeo Bimbi (1648–1730)

Sugolo When we come to making wine, which all our townsfolk do, and the grapes are brought in from the estates, we keep back large amounts of the must from the pressing. We boil this with flour until all the water has evaporated, to make *sugolo*. As the wagons of grapes come into town, all the artisans with no plot of land of their own come running up with pots and jars to beg for some of the must, which it would be shameful to refuse them. I can remember one gentleman who parted with over half his load in this way.

How very different from France and Germany, where the people very rarely let you eat any of the grapes, and as soon as they start to ripen post public watchmen to guard them day and night and punish anyone who so much as dares to pick one in passing. This could never happen in my country and, if it did, the amount of money saved would be totally insignificant. As it is, we not only let people help themselves to what they want, but any traveller has the right to eat grapes growing on the public highway, and take as much as he wants away with him as well, without the owner daring to complain. This I think must be derived from the Laws of Moses, which command that the farmer should leave every seventh sheaf of corn for the poor.

If growers in my region did not send barges piled high with their surplus wine to Venice, they would find themselves with more on their hands than they knew what to do with. In fact they often produce more wine than barrels to put it in, and sometimes end up giving it away in exchange for the empty barrel.

This reminds me of when I was a lad in Germany, where there was a rather delightful custom for marriageable young women to invite the neighbouring young men to help them with the grape harvest. I was in Basle at the time, among those invited by a charming young lady to gather her grapes. When she saw me eating some of them, she exclaimed in a peevish voice: 'Hey! Those are for making wine with, not for eating!'

The contrast with our own custom made me laugh. In Italy, if a stranger or peasant passes by without asking for some grapes, the harvesters take offence and shower them with abuse. They will give them away gladly, and thank you for taking them. And if a traveller in the intense heat asks these peasants for a drink of water, they reply: 'The water's rotting away in the ditch, friend, we

couldn't give you that, but if you'd like some wine, you'd be very welcome.' If he were alive today, my Lord Sir John North, father of the present baron, would recall how we were surprised and pleased when this happened to us in Brescia in 1575, when I was his tutor on a tour of the beauties of Italy.

Plums with nuts and jasmine. Giovanna Garzoni (1600–1670)

I have said nothing yet about the enormous quantities of grapes that we hang from the rafters, or keep fresh all winter in large boxes of new straw, not to mention the even larger amounts of raisins we dry in the sun or in ovens.

Plums start to be good about this time, but since they are known everywhere I don't need to say much about them, except that they are healthy to eat and better fresh than dried. They should only be eaten when fully ripe and during meals; not afterwards as you do in this country.

Plums or prunes

Arbutus

Next comes the berry which grows on the arbutus tree, known in Tuscany as *albatro*. A small tree, it flowers in July with little bell-shaped flowers clustered together like bunches of grapes alongside the fruit. This takes a year to ripen, turning from yellow to red, and is rather like a strawberry, only bigger. It tastes rather harsh and prickles the tongue and inside of the mouth. I do not remember ever seeing the arbutus outside Italy.

Then we have another noble fruit which is not yet known beyond the Alps. The azarole is beautiful to look at, delicious to eat, and good for you as well. It is grown from scions of red apples grafted on to the wild plum. The fruit is the size of a walnut, or smaller, and at first sight you would take it for a nice plump cherry. It has a sour-sweet taste, and is an incredibly effective thirst-quencher for patients suffering from a raging fever. Doctors use it to reduce fever.

Azarole

I should not forget to mention that six years ago I had the honour of introducing these fruits to Sir Henry Wotton in Venice when he was His Majesty's ambassador there. He liked them so much that he has eaten them ever since, whenever he can get them. He often used to say that he would give any amount of money to be able to send twenty-five of them home to England.

Quinces

There are three kinds of quince. The best is the apple quince, rather like a *chrisomele*, as it is sometimes called, because it is small and squat and divided into sections. It is yellow, downy and very much more fragrant than the other kinds. The second sort is much bigger and called 'pear quince' on account of its shape. It is more succulent and pulpy and not as good as the others, less downy and aromatic. The third kind is called 'bastard quince' because it is grafted on to another tree. Bastard quinces are bigger than apples and smaller than pears, and half-way between the two kinds in taste.

Above: Mattioli, New Kreüterbuch, *1563. Opposite: Oak tree and birds. Jacopo Ligozzi (1547–1627)*

All these three kinds are indispensable to the druggist because of their astringent properties. They are also used in wines and oils, and in the preparation of savouries, jellies, sweetmeats and quince

Quercus Robur, e Parus coeruleus,
Motacilla Troglodytes Fringilla coelebs

pastes, which are delights for all, not just for the sick.

For preserving, quinces should be really well ripened, otherwise they become hard and woody. We cook them in must and wine, with very ripe grapes and sugar, and we serve this preserve with the fruit at the end of a meal.

Branches of quinces trained against a wall make fine espaliers, and that concludes all I have to say about this noble fruit.

Medlars   Medlars are gathered at the end rather than the beginning of autumn. They ripen, as the proverb says, with a little time and a little straw. Medlars are quite well known in England, and well liked for their pleasant flavour. They are eaten raw after meals, with or without sugar.

Children are particularly fond of medlars because of their association with the feast of St Martin [the night of 10 November], which we call the *Ventura*. I must explain what this is all about. Just as the rulers of Italy in olden times established public amusements to keep the populace docile and entertained, our heads of households set aside certain days of innocent games and pastimes for their children, one of these being the *Ventura*. This is the night when the new wines are tasted and the order in which the wines should be drunk is established, and no one would tempt providence by broaching them before this ceremony. Hence the somewhat trite local saying:

> *A San Martino,*
> *ogni mosto è buon vino.*
>
> On St Martin's night we think
> any must is good to drink.

So on this night small children are not sent to bed before their parents, as they usually are in winter, when children under ten are in bed not long after sunset. (I have not noticed this excellent custom in any other country and I approve of it for several reasons. If young children don't dine with their elders, they don't risk eating more than is good for them, and the rest of the family, who have other things to think about, will not be bothered with their childish nonsense. And anyway, little creatures should be in bed early so as to get up in good time for school the next morning.)

And so, when this special evening arrives, the father of the family settles himself by the fire and has a basket brought to him. In it he puts as many pairs of medlars as there are people under his roof, and one extra for the poor. Then he covers the basket with a cloth so that he can hide three small coins in three of the fruit, gives the basket a good shake, and announces: 'Let it be known to one and all that I have put three coins inside these fruit – a *denaio*, a two-*denaio* piece and a *soldo*. Whoever finds the smallest of them shall win one *scudo*, the next size up wins one half of one, and the largest he keeps and gets a third of a *scudo* as well.'

Then he calls his youngest child to him and says: 'Put your hand into the basket and take out two medlars for the poor and put them on the table', making sure the child does not peep to see if they have any money in them. This continues until the child has distributed all the medlars, except the last two, which it keeps for itself. Then everyone looks inside their fruit, and if there is any money in the ones for the poor, it will be given to the first beggar who knocks on the door the next morning. Then follows a big celebration, tinged for some with sadness at not winning the *Ventura*, and with noisy merriment for others. I well remember the indescribable joy I once felt on finding the money in a fruit.

When this cheerful commotion has died down, the medlars are eaten and the wines sampled. There are so many wines to taste, that even though everyone takes only a sip, some of the party have been known to go up to bed somewhat merrier than usual, much to the delight of the rest of the family.

Medlars. Jacques le Moyne de Morgues (1530–88)

The jujube berry

These berries are edible, though not yet completely ripe, by the beginning of autumn, but they taste better when fully mature. Some find them quite indigestible and unhealthy, and I don't think they grow in England.

Olives

Then comes the olive harvest. They are picked before they are ripe and must be treated before they can be eaten. The oil is made from

Fruit market. Lucas van Valkenborch (1535–97)

ripe olives. Its health-giving qualities and many uses are so well known that I need not describe them here. Nor do I need to explain how to preserve olives, since you import them already prepared.

Sweet chestnuts   Next we have sweet chestnuts, which are so beneficial to mankind, but which you do not have here. They are good to eat raw or cooked, but cooked is best.

We roast chestnuts in a perforated dish over the fire and leave them for a while under hot ashes. Then we clean and peel them and eat them with salt and pepper.

Another way is to cook them on a grid over hot coals and cover them with ashes, as explained above, and eat them seasoned with orange juice rather than sugar, as you do here.

Many eat sweet chestnuts instead of medlars for the *Ventura* with a sip of wine after each one, which leaves them reeling if the wine is young and sweet.

Simply boiled in water they are food for peasants and young children rather than discriminating adults.

We also cook chestnuts in good-quality sweet white wine, and when they are done strain them and put them to dry in the smoke. They are marvellous preserved this way, and last for a whole year.

Even larger quantities of chestnuts are dried and smoked, uncooked, in baskets, and then shelled by putting them in sacks and bashing them. They will last for two years or more.

When roses are in bloom our ladies take quantities of these dried chestnuts and mix them with rose petals in coffers and baskets, where the chestnuts soon become soft and very fragrant.

We make bread out of flour made from the smaller ones, which tastes sweet, and is far from insipid. This flour will keep well for several years, so our rulers keep great stores of it in their fortresses as wartime provisions. Once dried it deteriorates very little.

The poor are well-nourished on dried chestnuts and cook them in various ways. Some stew them with vegetables such as beans or grass peas. Others soak them, remove the inner skin and cook them until soft, and then mix them with *ricotta* or cream, which is really very nice.

Peeled chestnuts are used with prunes, raisins and breadcrumbs in a stuffing for roast chicken, goose or turkey.

Chestnuts are the main food for thousands in our mountainous regions, who hardly ever see wheat bread. When the chestnut crop is poor, and the price of wheat high, they suffer a great deal. So long as they have plenty of chestnuts and milk, bread and wine means nothing to them, and yet they are fine, robust people.

Christ in the house of Martha and Mary (detail). Pieter Aertsen (1508/9–75)

Sorb-apples or service fruit

Sorb-apples are picked at the beginning of autumn while they are still sharp, and put to ripen in straw or hung in bunches from nails. They have the same taste as medlars but are very astringent and not so pleasant. They are dried for use in Lent, and made into a preserve with sugar, which is excellent for dysentery.

The wood from the tree is hard and red, and carpenters make their tools from it, as well as household things and pretty inlays.

Cornelian cherries

Cornelian cherries are good now. They are a little red fruit, longish in shape and as big as a medium-sized olive. They have very hard stones, a bitter flavour and are even more astringent than sorb-apples. This is not what I call a serious fruit; it is more for little children and pregnant women than grown men. The preserve is even more effective for dysentery than the sorb preserve.

Water chestnuts

These grow in freshwater canals which are not too fast-flowing, like the Brenta, which carries the barge traffic from Padua to Venice. The water chestnut is a plant with broad, round leaves and a white flower similar to a lily. It produces a sort of hard fruit with a deep brown shell like a chestnut, triangular or four-sided, with sharp edges.

These are cooked in salted water and have something of the taste of chestnuts, but are not so nice. They are therefore more suitable for brute beasts than men. Since the plant is of the cold humour, one assumes that its fruit would be both cold and windy.

Carobs

There grows in the Kingdom of Naples a tall tree as big as an oak which bears a fruit called carob. In their unripe state, you might think that they were broad bean pods, but rather flat and not so round.

When dried, carob pods are the colour of chestnuts and taste rather sweet. They are sweeter, however, when green. Inside are hard little nuts of the same colour. Carobs are said to be highly indigestible, but heated over hot coals and eaten after meals, they will clear up catarrh. They have many other beneficial effects.

Water chestnuts.
Jacques le Moyne
de Morgues
(1530–88)

We seem to have more pomegranates than formerly. They are a very good fruit on their own, and make an excellent seasoning for cooked dishes.

    They are a particularly good restorative for invalids. The juice assuages the violent thirst of the feverish. We make a beautiful-looking wine from its pretty seeds for that purpose.

Pomegranates

Next we have nuts from the stone pine. These delicate kernels, safely tucked away in their little cells, are delicious eaten raw on their own, or with bread, or put in the stuffing for a chicken. They are very nutritious and increase men's supply of sperm. They are made into comfits with sugar, or coated with sugar like almonds; they are also put into pastries and delicious little tarts.

Pine nuts

Still life with pomegranate. Giovanna Garzoni (1600–1670)

127

Mushrooms   Although mushrooms are found in spring and summer, I decided to describe them here because they are most plentiful in autumn. In fact they are as abundant here in England as they are in Italy, though few people seem to know much about them.

Field mushrooms   So called because they grow in fields and meadows, these come in the spring and are small and very white, with pink, hard insides. They are very good and not a bit harmful. To eat them, simply peel off the delicate outer skin and boil them a little, press them dry between two cloths, flour and fry them and serve them with salt, pepper and bitter orange juice.

Another way is to cook field mushrooms gently in a saucepan with a little water, plenty of oil or butter, garlic, salt, pepper and a decent amount of sweet herbs. Serve them sprinkled with bitter orange juice, or a little verjuice or vinegar. Whoever eats them like this and doesn't lick their fingers does not, in my opinion, know much about true gluttony.

Ovali   These egg-shaped mushrooms appear in woods and fields in the summer, especially when it has rained after a long drought. When the white peel has been removed they are almost scarlet. They are extremely good, and considered some of the best. Although they are quite harmless, it is best to be on the safe side and boil them first, cut into pieces, in water with salt and a little garlic, making sure that they are completely submerged in the boiling water. This draws out any harmful substances, which can then be drained away, leaving the mushrooms free of poison. Boiled like this, the *ovali* can then be fried or stewed as explained in the previous recipes. The stalks, if they are not wormy, are just as good as the rest of the mushroom.

Parasol mushrooms   These mushrooms come at the end of summer; they are very wide on a long, thin stem. Some are white on the outside and reddish on the inside, but not as firm or tightly closed as the field mushrooms; others are a very dark, chestnut brown. All of them should have a ring in the middle of the stalk, a reliable indication that they are safe, but without which they are harmful.

Parasol mushrooms are good cooked as described above. They can be preserved for Lent, after the first boil, by putting them in a glazed pot with layers of salt, starting with about half an inch of salt, followed by a layer of carefully drained and dried mushrooms, and so on until the pot is full, making sure the last layer is salt, which is then covered with a plate under a heavy weight. The

Still life with ovali *mushrooms.*
Giacomo Fardella

mushrooms will keep a long time this way; as long as you wish. To use them, they are soaked overnight in tepid water, then washed, dried, and floured, and fried in oil or butter, and served with a little garlic, pepper and bitter orange juice.

Boletus mushrooms These do not appear until the end of autumn or early winter and are found in ancient woods of beech or chestnut, more often in the mountains than on the plains. They are quite big and solid, the colour of a russet apple, round in shape when seen from above, with big thick stems. They are the best of all for salting. They are greatly esteemed, whether eaten fresh or salted.

Polmoneschi This somewhat strange mushroom grows on the trunks or the roots of trees, especially oak. I do not know their real name, but since they resemble lungs, being about the same size and colour, and are spongy, I call them *polmoneschi*. I can assure you that they are really delicious to eat, boiled or fried as described above. When they have been left to harden on the tree, we use them to light the fire on winter nights.

Sponge mushrooms So called because they are full of tiny holes, like a sponge, these mushrooms appear in the spring, although they are more plentiful in the autumn. They are shaped like little pyramids on their stalks, which are also good to eat. Simply washed and cooked in the usual way, they are like ordinary mushrooms, and in no way harmful.

The mushroom stone There are many other kinds of mushroom, of varying quality, whose names do not immediately come to mind. It would be very remiss of me not to mention the Roman ones. These are like little stones, but not so hard. Buried in a terracotta pot full of best garden soil and watered every evening, these will produce fifteen or twenty mushrooms by the next morning, not very large, admittedly, but wholesome and good. When I was living in Modena I had one brought for me, and grew mushrooms from it all summer; it is hard to believe this unless one has actually experienced it.

In Rome they call these mushrooms *fongaruola*, and many fine lords and cardinals have pots of them on their windowsills, and derive no small pleasure from watering and picking the mushrooms with their own fair hands.

Just a few days ago in Eltham Park, we were returning home from church on Sunday morning, and as we passed through the park gates Sir Adam Newton's little girl called out to me: 'There's a nice flower for you, Castelvetro!' Turning to where she was pointing, I saw on one of the pillars a magnificent mushroom, even more beautiful than the ones I have just described, as yellow as gold, and hard, and so ingeniously formed by nature that it was a delight to behold. I immediately rushed up and picked it, whereupon Lady Newton, who was one of the party, asked me what I meant to do with it. I said I intended to eat it. 'You won't get me to try any!' she cried. 'All the better for me, my Lady, for then I shall have so much more of it,' I replied.

It so happened that after lunch that afternoon I had to go to London, so I took the mushroom with me and ate it the next day and found it excellent, my only suffering being sadness when it was all gone.

The mushroom without a name

Celery

Celery is good at the beginning of this beautiful season. Its seeds, which are extremely small, are sown in early spring in sifted ashes. When the stalks are a foot high, they need to be planted out about seven inches apart, for they grow quite large heads. They should be sown at sunset in good, rich soil, and watered often if the weather is dry. In early autumn the celery plants are dug up and earthed up close together in a trench about a yard deep, with the tops showing about four fingers above the earth, and left for fifteen to twenty days. They will then have blanched and become good to eat.

To eat celery, dig up the required amount and wash it well, and serve it raw with salt and pepper after meals. It is warm, and has great digestive and generative powers, and for this reason young wives often serve celery to their elderly or impotent husbands.

Pumpkins or gourds

I almost forgot to mention the different kinds of gourds, which are at their best in the autumn. Their popular name is 'marine pumpkins', perhaps because they are used by inexperienced swimmers, scared of drowning, who strap a whole dried gourd under their chests, to keep from sinking into the sea. Small children learn to swim in the rivers with them.

Some gourds are green, some green and yellow, some long, some broad, while others are all white and round and flat, which are the best for the noble art of swimming. The green ones, the first to be ready, start to be good to eat about midsummer, when they are the size of a large apple.

Gourds are cooked in the same way as marrows. They are also good cut up very small, or in strips the size of your little finger, floured, fried, and served with salt, pepper and bitter orange juice.

The small ones can be cooked whole in salted water, then cut up and put in a covered pot with melted butter and salt and pepper and left to soak up the flavours. Everyone enjoys them this way.

We make a really tasty, nourishing dish from the big ones. First

Still life with musical instruments. Munari

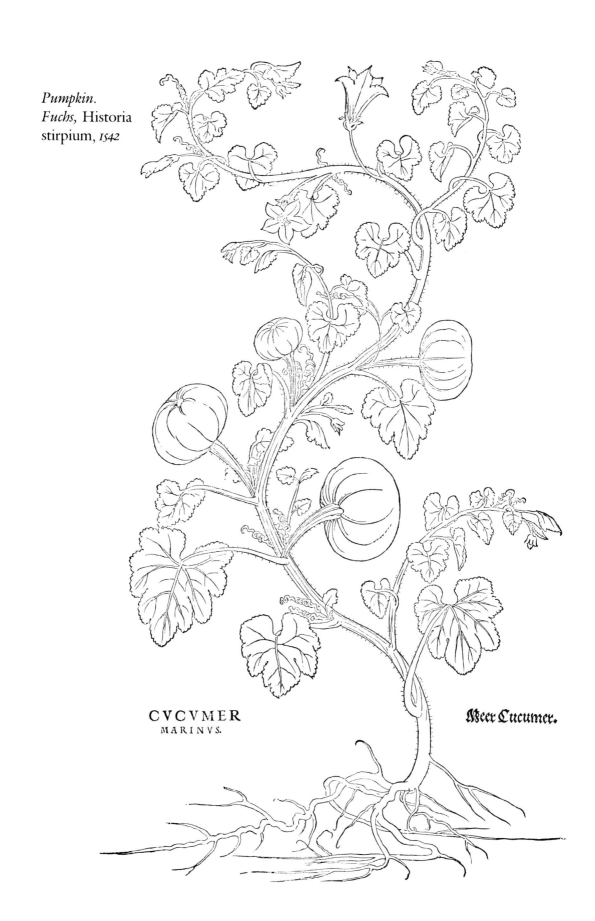

Pumpkin.
Fuchs, Historia
stirpium, *1542*

CVCVMER
MARINVS.

Meer Cucumer.

cook them in good broth and then, when almost done, thicken the liquid with a mixture of white breadcrumbs, rich mature cheese, strong spices or ground pepper, and two or three well-beaten eggs.

This recipe works well, too, with the remains of a melon: carefully pare away the outer rind, and prepare as above.

In winter we make good pies from these gourds or pumpkins. The white ones, when cut into very thin slices and dried, look exactly like the most exquisite kid gloves, and I once tricked some ladies into thinking that this was what they had just eaten. They laughed a lot at my little joke.

Pumpkin shoots

And now, having written all there is to be said about the abundant fruits and vegetables of this season, I need only describe the shoots of pumpkins, which wind their way up trees and hedges and along the ground. Cut them off about seven inches long, including the two small leaves with a little bud between them, and if there are any tiny gourds as well, so much the better, for these will improve the flavour. Washed, and tied in bundles of about twenty, they are cooked in a capacious pan as a described for mallow shoots, but take great care that they do not disintegrate in cooking, or the tips, which are the best part, will fall off and be left behind in the pan. Drain them well and dress them with olive oil, salt and pepper.

Kitchen scene (detail). David Teniers the Younger (1610–90)

Winter

At the beginning of this dismal season, we use the green leaves of chicory in salads; the tenderest leaves are chopped finely with garlic, which we always eat with chicory, and added to the salad.

At the same time we have the shoots of the chicory plant, which are buried in sand to make them white and crisp.

The roots are also eaten; first they have to be scraped carefully with a knife, then cut down the middle and the woody and unpleasant core, its 'soul', as we call it, removed. They are then boiled and cut into pieces and seasoned like other salads, but with the addition of some well-washed raisins to mitigate their wholesome bitterness.

Chicory

For a good part of this season we also have white endive, which I have already described. Since it is well enough known in this country, I need say no more here.

White endive

Then we have watercress, the last green salad of the season, which goes on being available all winter provided the streams are not frozen. It makes quite a pleasant salad, but since there is no alternative it always seems better than it really is. Because watercress grows in fast-running water it is very refreshing and is usually eaten raw.

Watercress

I once happened to be in France in the company of a group of ladies and gentlemen, and we came one afternoon to a large village

Cabbage salad

137

with a good inn, where we proposed to dine. One of the ladies, sitting in the window-seat of the dining-room, which overlooked an orchard, said to me, 'Let's go into the garden and pick a salad!' to which I replied, 'Yes, indeed!' When we got there we found nothing but cabbages, so the young lady picked one of these saying, 'Well if there's nothing else, I'll make you all a nice salad out of this.'

Having never seen or eaten anything like this before, I kept silent and waited for the outcome. First she removed the green outer leaves until she came to the white part, which she proceeded to slice very finely with a razor-sharp knife. She then salted and dressed it in the usual way, and brought it to the table, where it was pronounced excellent, and her ingenuity was much admired by the entire company.

Cooked onions When there are no spring onions, we make a salad of roasted onions seasoned with crushed pepper. This is tastier and more wholesome than eating them boiled.

Onions without pepper are excellent for clearing up the sort of bad cough that lingers after a cold.

Carrots We prepare salads from pink and yellow carrots, roasted or boiled in the same way, and turnips as well. They all need pepper as the most important seasoning.

Turnips We make an excellent dish with turnips, different from the way you do here; they are first peeled, then cut into thin slices and cooked in good broth, and served with grated cheese and pepper.

Fruit We eat more or less the same kinds of apples and pears in winter as in the autumn. The same applies to fresh grapes, which, as I have explained, we preserve by hanging from the rafters.

Truffles So I shall say no more about these, but go on to talk of truffles, as

Kitchen equipment. Bartolomeo Scappi, *Epulario*, 1570

Winter. Sebastian Stoskopff
(1596/9–1657)

more appropriate to the season, although they can be found somewhat earlier, and indeed in many regions of Italy.

Botanists tell us that this noble fruit is a kind of mushroom, which grows hidden underground and never sees the light of day. Some people go hunting truffles out of gluttony, and some are greedy for money, and they have two ways of searching for them. When the ground is covered in snow, there sometimes appears on the surface a tiny, bright yellow plant which peasants know conceals truffles, hidden about five or six inches underground.

Our poet Petrarch, comparing the eyes of his beloved to the rays of the sun, said in his nineteenth sonnet, which begins *'Quando il pianeta che ...'*:

E non pur quel che s'apre a noi di fore
le rive e i colli di fioretti adorna,
ma dentro, dove gia mai non s'aggiorna,
gravido fa di sé il terrestre umore,
onde tal frutto e simile si colga . . .

Nor that glow which lights up
Hills and dales with little flowers,
But cannot penetrate the earth,
Which, pregnant by itself alone,
Produces this fruit so rare . . .

'This fruit so rare' has been interpreted as a dish of truffles the poet was intending to send to a friend.

The other way of finding truffles is by means of that dirty animal, the pig, who loves them more than anything else, and whose acute sense of smell leads it to where they are hidden. The aroma of truffles is rather like that of mushrooms, but much stronger, so the pig can find them however deep the snow is. It digs with its snout into the earth under the snow, and would devour the truffles straight away, but for the wily peasant, who keeps a sharp eye on the pig and when it finds some, drives it away with his spade and grabs the truffles for himself.

The biggest truffles are about the size of an egg; but some are as big as a quince. Truffles are not as spongy as mushrooms. There are two kinds; one has black flesh, like charcoal, and the other is pale. Both of them have a rough, black skin. The black truffles are the best and the most expensive. They sell for more than half a golden *scudo* the pound. They are mainly found around Rome. The pale ones cost less, and large quantities are to be had in Lombardy.

Truffles should be wrapped in damp paper and cooked in the ashes for about a quarter of an hour. Then peel them just as you would a baked apple or pear, cut them up very small, and finish cooking them in a pan with oil, salt and pepper. When they are nice and hot the truffles are ready to eat, and they are good to eat as they are, with just some lemon or bitter orange juice.

Still life. Juan
Sánchez Cotán
(1561–1637)

Truffles will keep for a whole year. This is how it is done: after roasting them in the ashes, peel your truffles and cut them into small pieces. Put them in a little pot of olive oil, so that all the pieces are completely covered, and then close it tightly. Store the pot in a dry place. When you need some, take out as many as you want, and heat them in a pan with fresh oil, salt and pepper. Don't forget to serve them with a squeeze of lemon or bitter orange juice – they need nothing else.

With truffles I come to the end of my description of the fruit, herbs, and vegetables of Italy. It would be appropriate for me to finish with an amusing little incident concerning truffles that occurred during my first journey away from home.

In the year of our Lord 1572 I found myself in Germany, studying the somewhat cumbersome language of that noble nation. I was living in the village of Rotteln in Baden Baden, about three miles outside the beautiful city of Basle, which was so full of students from Italy, France and Spain that I had been unable to find lodgings there.

One day I was invited to dine with the lord of that village and the surrounding countryside. The company consisted of a group of gentlemen, one of whom, a charming young baron, had just returned from a visit to Italy. When he heard where I was from, he said, 'Can you tell me, my friend, since you are Italian, why it is that the noblemen of the most civilized nation in the world perambulate their estates in the company of pigs?'

I assumed that he must have seen someone out hunting truffles, in the way I have just described, and could not help laughing at his bewilderment. He took this in bad part, as if I had been calling him a liar or making fun of him. 'Well,' he said crossly, 'is it true, or isn't it?' So to placate him I quickly replied, 'You are absolutely right, you may well have seen quite a few of these gentlemen walking along behind a pig, tied to one of its back legs with a piece of string. But you must also have noticed that the gentleman was followed by a peasant with a spade or shovel over his shoulder.' 'Well, yes, that's true,' he said, 'but there they all were, out walking with pigs.'

'What you saw,' I went on, 'was not an Italian nobleman leading his pig to pasture, but a gentleman following his pig on a treasure hunt. And great fun it is, too. The pig has a keen sense of smell, without which it would never be able to find the treasure, which is hidden deep in the ground under the snow. If you had waited long enough you would have seen the animal rootling in the ground with its snout, and the gentleman pulling the pig back, while the peasant dug away with his spade.'

The young nobleman replied, 'Now that I understand what was

Man with pig.
Stefano della Bella
(1610–64)

going on, I am no longer scandalized by such behaviour, and am very much obliged to you. But I still cannot imagine what on earth it was that they could have been searching for. If you do not mind, I should be vastly obliged to you for an explanation.'

'Well,' I replied, 'the treasure is not a lump of earth, as some people think, but a sort of mushroom that grows in the ground and never shows above it, called *tartufo.*'

When he heard its name, so like the German *der Teufel* (which means 'devil'), he said, 'Good heavens, how can you bear to eat that sort of monster!' At which I could not prevent myself from laughing out loud, and said, 'I wish to God we had some of these little devils here today, for I am sure that you and all the present company would enjoy them enormously.'

'Well, I must confess,' he said, 'I can well believe that, for I remember how I used to refuse to eat frogs and snails, when I was in your country. I thought they were quite repellent, and now I enjoy them so much I eat them the way other people do chickens or partridges.'

146

He then went on to talk of other things, and our conversation came to an end. Later he very courteously invited me to visit him. I was entertained on several occasions in his beautiful castle, delightfully situated on a nearby hilltop. There he would offer me exquisitely prepared frogs, and we would both laugh heartily at our little misunderstanding.

*The End
of the account of
the Fruit, Herbs & Vegetables
that are eaten
in Italy.*

*Written out on the 28th day of September
in the village of Charlton
in England.*
MDCXIV

Fruit market. Lucas van Valkenborch (1535–97)

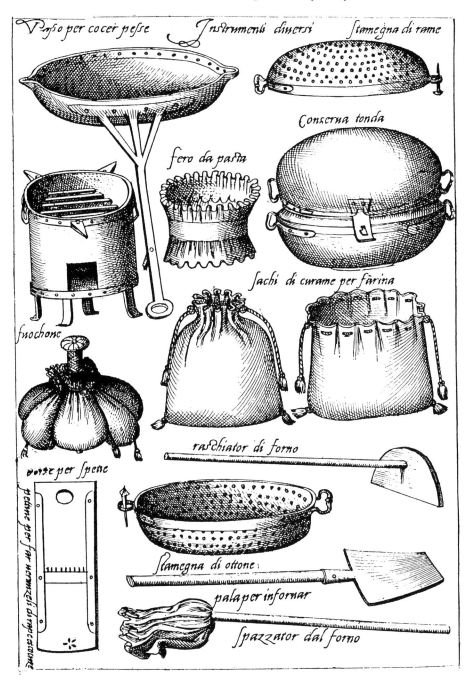

Vaso per cocer pesse

Instrumenti diuersi

stamegna di rame

Conserua tonda

fero da pasta

fuochone

sachi di curame per farina

raschiator di forno

vasse per spexe

stamegna di ottone

pala per infornar

spazzator dal forno

Glossary & Notes

Agliata is a sauce made from peeled and skinned walnuts pounded in a mortar with garlic and salt, and thinned to the required consistency with stock, cream or lemon juice. It is similar to the Middle Eastern *tarator* sauce. It may have been introduced to Europe by the Arabs, but in countries where nuts were a plentiful local crop the idea of using them to thicken sauces and stews probably developed independently.

Agresto is the slightly fermented juice of unripe grapes, used as a souring agent or for seasoning dishes instead of vinegar or lemon juice. The English version of this was **verjuice**, made from sour apples as well as grapes. Sometimes Castelvetro just squeezes a handful of unripe grapes into a stew or over a salad.

Alexanders has a flavour rather like celery and grows wild in Britain. The shoots, leaves and stems were all used as flavourings or as a vegetable. It has been superseded by celery and is hard to come by nowadays.

Almonds were used in ways familiar to us, in marzipan and almond paste, in England as well as Italy, but Castelvetro also reminds us of their use in almond butter and almond milk. These were not unknown, though, in early-seventeenth-century England – they are described in *Elinor Fettiplace's Receipt Book*,* and the editor, Hilary Spurling, gives clear versions of how to make them today.

*See Bibliography.

When in a hurry, with no time to shell, peel and grind almonds in the correct way, I use commercial ground almonds to thicken the juices of baked fish or meat. This is a delicious alternative to flour- or cream-based sauces, but must be used thoughtfully, for the almonds can swamp some delicate flavours.

In Castelvetro's time shelled but unpeeled almonds were pounded up and used in sauces; the skins gave the sauce a brown colour, but did not spoil the flavour.

Green almonds can be eaten shell and all; the flavour is rather sharp and fruity. A half-eaten one can be seen in the illustration on p. 20.

Apples: sadly, we have no commercial equivalents today of the varieties of apple described by Castelvetro. Bland Coxes and crisp, tasteless Golden Delicious do not have the aromas and sharpness of the many traditional apples which are now difficult to find.

I once strayed into an abandoned orchard in Herefordshire and every windfall I tasted was an explosion of flavour – sharp, sweet, perfumed – and all different. It is a good idea on country walks to look out for wild crab apples and escapes from gardens and orchards and try using them in sweet and savoury dishes. They are a good addition to fruit jellies.

Castelvetro writes of the *paradiso* apple being used to perfume ointments. In addition, apple juice has a tonic, toning effect on the skin, hence the name 'pomade', from the French *pomme*.

Apricots are transformed when dried or preserved in sugar. They develop a rich aroma and a dense texture and can be used in savoury as well as sweet dishes. Dried apricot paste, sold in paper-thin sheets, is a useful source of energy and vitamin A and can be whizzed with water in the blender to make the delicious Middle Eastern apricot drink, *qamar al din*. In Italy the kernels are made into a liqueur and also used to flavour bitter-sweet macaroons, *amaretti*, which are used, crumbled, in sweet and savoury dishes, like pumpkin ravioli or dried vegetable purées.

Arbutus is a juicy, red fruit on a bush or small tree, also known as the strawberry tree, which grows wild all over the Mediterranean, and in south-west Ireland. It is also grown as an ornamental tree in gardens in the milder parts of England.

Asparagus is used in Italian regional cooking in many inventive ways which makes dunking them messily in melted butter seem quite barbaric. Castelvetro's use of olive oil and bitter orange juice as a dressing is lighter and more delicious. Asparagus is excellent served with a little butter and grated Parmesan, melted briefly under the grill.

The bones and horns Castelvetro instructs us to use in preparing an asparagus bed provide a slow release of nitrogenous fertilizer into the soil, similar to hoof and horn meal.

Azarole, *Crataegus azarolus*, was introduced into Italy from the Middle East in Roman times. The fruit is eaten ripe, and used in jams and jellies.

Bitter orange juice is a delicious alternative to lemon juice on meat or fish, or with a cooked vegetable salad. Although sweet oranges were available in Castelvetro's Italy, their juice would not have been used in this way. The aroma of both the juice and the peel of bitter oranges is much more aromatic. You can have a supply of this all the year round by buying in a crate of Seville oranges when they come into the shops briefly in January and February. After making a year's supply of marmalade there will still be plenty of oranges left to squeeze out the juice to freeze in the ice-cube box. Scrape in some peel as well, and store the orange cubes in plastic bags in the freezer. They can be used in salad dressings, sauces, popped inside the cavity of duck before roasting, added to Mexican and Latin American recipes, and put into drinks (vodka or *martini rosso* or rum). The peel can be frozen separately to use where the aroma but not the acidity is needed – it is excellent in chocolate cakes and spiced buns.

Broad beans have been around in Europe since the Stone Age. They are a different variety from the other beans mentioned by Castelvetro, which were relatively new arrivals, brought in from the New World during the previous century and assimilated much more rapidly than the potato and the tomato. Our name 'French bean' reminds us of the French presence in North and South America. Castelvetro describes runner beans as 'Turkish', meaning exotic or foreign. They did not originate in Turkey.

These beans caught on because they were an easy crop, content with poor soil, and useful to grow in the fields between main crops. They could be eaten fresh and young, shelled or in their pods, and kept, dried, for use through the winter. Castelvetro's instructions for cooking dried beans are precise and in line with what we now know about the dangers of eating undercooked beans. (They contain harmful cyanogens which can be destroyed by boiling, uncovered, in water.) He tells us to throw away the water after the first boiling and then simmer them in fresh water, only then adding salt and seasonings.

Broccoli in Castelvetro's time was not a specialized crop like calabrese, but the little shoots which grew on the stalks of cabbages and cauliflowers left in the garden over the winter. The addition of chopped garlic when cooking broccoli is a great improvement.

Broth is how I translate *brodo* – the word 'stock' has been debased by commercial stock cubes. Castelvetro would have used the liquid from simmering joints of meat and chickens to enrich his vegetable dishes, except in Lent and on 'lean' days, when water or the liquid from cooking dried pulses would have been used.

Cabbages have been selectively cultivated for thousands of years and contemporary paintings show marvellous specimens, some a great deal larger than the ones we buy today. Castelvetro's cabbage recipes are superb.

Cabbage water, or a decoction sweetened with honey, is an old folk remedy for bronchial complaints, and a poultice made of cabbage leaves would relieve lumbago and sharp pains like the 'stitch'. Castelvetro recommends a powder made from dried cabbage stalks for this purpose.

Carob pods can be chewed for their earthy sweetish flavour and are often used in confectionery and biscuits. They can sometimes be found in health-food shops and ethnic stores.

Chickpeas, one of the most ancient of the cultivated pulses, are excellent cooked as Castelvetro describes, simmered in water with oil, herbs and garlic; the liquid can be thickened by crushing some towards the end of cooking. Tinned chickpeas are good, but do not always have the nuttiness of those cooked at home. Some good brands of Italian tinned chickpeas are flavoured with sage leaves.

Cornel, **cornelian cherry** or **dogwood**, *Cornus mas*, does grow in this country, but the berries rarely ripen, or are eaten by birds if they do. We are more familiar with the yellow flowers, but the fruit makes nice jam and jelly.

Cucumbers need to have more flavour than the large, juicy, crisp, but tasteless ones generally on sale here today if you want to use them cooked. Turkish or Cypriot ones, small and less watery, are better. They have more body and so are also good when chopped or grated into yoghurt salads.

Druggists or pharmacists supplied medicines prescribed by doctors, and also spices, sugar and confectionery. In the Venetian Republic their activities were strictly controlled and offenders against the law were publicly burnt on the Rialto. The adulteration of spices and medicines was widespread, which is probably why Castelvetro tells us to use crushed, not powdered, pepper to season many of his dishes.

Fat dishes, see **Lean dishes**.

Fennel has been used in the kitchen since Roman times, the seeds as a spice, the young leaves as a herb and the bulbs and stems as a vegetable, eaten raw or cooked. The wild variety was bitter, compared with the sweet cultivated strains. The flavours of these three parts of the plant are very different. The raw bulb is crisp and aromatic, good to eat at the start of a meal, and, as Castelvetro points out, it improves the taste of wine drunk with it. When cooked it has a much milder flavour: coarsely chopped fennel, simmered in a very little moisture and its own juices, and then liquidized with *crème fraîche*, Parmesan and the cooking juices of the fish, makes a wonderful sauce for baked fish.

Figs: the flowers grow inside a fleshy receptacle which, when fertilized, swells and becomes the fruit. Castelvetro was not correct in distinguishing between the first and second crop, which are both true fruits.

Gooseberries were preferred sour in Italy, and used in sauces for rich food like goose and pork, though Castelvetro liked them on chicken and veal as well. The English had recently taken to the idea, but seemed to prefer gooseberries in sweets and preserves. They even added sugar to the sour sauce for fowl.

Grass peas grew wild in Italy and were eaten a lot by the Romans, but have fallen out of use, which is just as well, as they are poisonous, even after a preliminary roasting, which is no doubt why they were said to generate 'wind, bad blood and considerable melancholy'.

Honey was the source of sweetness for most people from prehistoric times, but was being superseded by the more expensive sugar in seventeenth-century Europe. It would have been an ideal preservative for the graft Castelvetro took from a fine pear tree in Denmark; the scion could be cut in the autumn and kept until the spring, and then grafted on to the root stock at precisely the right moment.

Hops: the tender young shoots of the wild hop plant have been eaten since prehistoric times in Europe. They were eaten as a vegetable in the West Riding of Yorkshire when I was a child. We picked the young shoots from wild hop plants in the hedgerows, boiled them and ate them with bacon fat or butter. Thanks to the generosity of Kent Museum of Rural Life I have been able to try out some hop recipes; cooked briefly in their own juices they are delicious served warm with butter and garlic, or tepid with light olive oil and bitter orange juice. When hops were grown as a crop in Kent, from the seventeenth century onwards, the young shoots were eaten in the same way. Young nettles were eaten too, to cleanse the blood after a winter without fresh greenery.

Humours: the doctrine of the four humours was derived from ancient Greek medicine and was the basis of medical theory throughout the Middle Ages. According to this doctrine, all living things have a combination of characteristics, or humours: hot, cold, dry and wet. Their 'temperament' depends on the mixture of these humours. Illness is caused by the balance being wrong, and medicines were composed of a mixture of substances, plant, animal or mineral, which would correct this imbalance. A good doctor, or healer, would prescribe a treatment appropriate to the 'temperament' of the patient. The materials used by the cook and the pharmacist were described in terms of their degree of 'hotness' or 'coldness' or whatever. It was important for the cook to know the characteristics of the foodstuffs he was using, so that he could season them according to the requirements of his master's 'temperament'. The theory would be applied pragmatically – 'Always put some raw onion in a salad of purslane' – 'Never cook broccoli without some chopped garlic' – and many of our traditional recipes and food habits probably derive from applications of the long-forgotten theory of humours.

Jujube berries are still used, dried, in Middle Eastern cooking to give a fruity sourness to savoury dishes. They are the fruit of a spiny shrub which grows in the Mediterranean region. The berries are dark red or almost black when ripe, and about the size of an olive.

Lean dishes were eaten in Lent and on the days when the Roman Catholic church banned the use of meat and fowl, eggs and dairy produce. Fish, oil, almond milk and almond butter were used instead. This prohibition stimulated the inventiveness of cooks in rich households, but the diet of the poor must have been largely a lean one anyway. Castelvetro does not give any recipes using fish, except for oysters in pies, which is odd for someone who lived for twelve years in Venice. His lean dishes are delicious and would be acceptable to vegans.

Lemons were used in many of Castelvetro's recipes. They were readily available in seventeenth-century Italy.

When using lemon juice in Castelvetro's recipes we must ask ourselves what we want it to do. Is it for sourness or for its aroma? To cut the richness of a fatty, cloying sauce, or to perfume a dish right at the end of cooking? The traditional Italian mixture of finely chopped garlic, parsley and grated lemon peel – *gremolata* – added to a dish just before serving is crisp and fresh, and less drastic than a flood of acid juice. If you cannot get hold of really fresh, aromatic lemons it is better to do without altogether, or use one of the alternatives described under the entry for *agresto*.

Lettuce: the two kinds mentioned by Castelvetro can both be eaten cooked, braised, stewed or grilled over charcoal. There is no point in trying this with the tasteless varieties on sale today. Look for outdoor-grown Webb's Wonder or Cos.

Cos lettuces were blanched by tying the leaves together round a cane. This was still done until quite recently, but we now have selected strains which are self-blanching.

Lupin: the dried bean of the lupin plant. When prepared according to Castelvetro's instructions they have a pleasant, nutty flavour, to which enthusiasts become addicted.

They have been grown in Italy and the Middle East since Roman times, and are still cultivated for forage and much enjoyed as a ubiquitous street food.

An Egyptian friend, who cannot live without this snack, always brings her own supply to London, where her daughter's kitchen is invaded by bowls of lupin beans being purged under dripping taps. She does not eat them raw, as Castelvetro describes, but cooks them several times in salted water to draw off the remaining bitterness. This is just as well, as the bitterness is probably due to poisonous alkaloids.

It is not the foliage of lupins which makes good manure, but the white nodules on the roots which, when ploughed into the soil, provide it with nitrogen from the air in an assimilable form.

Medlars look rather peculiar and attract ribald names on account of the appearance of the aperture into which the coins were inserted for the St Martin's night ceremonies. They should be eaten well ripened, almost rotted. Although medlars do grow in England, the ones we buy in the shops usually come from Greece or Cyprus.

Millet originated in India but was known in Europe in prehistoric times. We know it only in bird food, but in Castelvetro's time the grain was used to make porridges and stews, the flour in bread and polenta.

Minestra: the literal translation is 'soup', but in the context in which Castelvetro and other sixteenth- and seventeenth-century writers use it, I prefer to say 'stew' or 'dish', a term which covers a whole range of recipes, not all of them liquid.

Mulberries: the dark fruit is delicious, with a sharp, sweet flavour, but so perishable that it is not a commercial crop. White mulberries, whose leaves are fed to silkworms, are often found in parts of the world where there was once a flourishing silk industry. They are cloying and insipid. They can be bought, dried, in Turkish stores in London.

Mushrooms: the 'mushroom without a name' was probably *Laetiporus sulphureus*, sulphur shelf or chicken of the woods, which when cooked is said to resemble chicken breast or tofu. It does not grow in northern Italy, so Castelvetro did not have a name for it, but he may have met it in Germany or France and was pleased to find it growing at Eltham.

Parasol mushrooms are one of the *Lepiota* species. Castelvetro was optimistic, though, in saying that the presence of a ring would indicate they were safe to eat; a more precise identification is needed.

Ovali are *Amanita caesarea*, known in Italy since antiquity.

Boletus mushrooms are the *funghi porcini* widely available in Italian food stores. They are used in many north Italian dishes, to savour stews and soups and in fillings for *tortelli*. During the war they were gathered and dried, and, together with dried chestnuts, were sometimes the only food to see families through the winter.

Sponge mushrooms were probably morels.

The mushroom stone is the pseudosclerotium of a centrally stalked bracket fungus called *Polyporus tuberaster*. It consists, not of coagulated wolf urine, as was once supposed, but of the mycelium of the mushroom bound up with a mixture of earth and pebbles, which resembles porous rock. These 'stones' were once quite common in the region around Naples, and it is typical of Castelvetro that he should have got hold of one and succeeded in growing mushrooms from it.

Musk is an aroma derived from the abdominal glands of animals, the most prized being a species of deer in the Himalayas. A similar flavouring, sometimes used to adulterate this perfume, comes from the seeds of a plant of the hibiscus family found in Egypt, *habb-al-musk*. The roots of a fern, *Polypodium vulgare*, have a similar flavour, and so do muscat grapes. It is likely that the aromatic seeds were what was used to give a musk flavour to medieval Arab dishes.

Must is the unfermented juice of ripe grapes. This was used in many ways apart from making wine. Its sweetness made it a cheap substitute for honey or that expensive condiment, sugar.

Boiled to a syrup, must was the preservative element in sweet pickles of fruit or vegetables, still manufactured today as *mostarda di frutta*, which is where we get the name 'mustard' for a similar pickle using *senape* or mustard seeds.

Boiled until it is reduced to a sticky paste, sometimes with the addition of dried grapes, must becomes the Turkish *pekmez*, which can be bought in Turkish stores in north London. It is delicious stirred into yoghurt. An interesting version is flavoured with ground sesame seeds. A less delicious *pekmez*, made with carob pods, was probably known to Castelvetro.

Olla podrida is the name Castelvetro gives to a mixed salad, to which two kinds of capers, ox tongue, olives, candied peel, raisins, angelica and so forth are added. This is the Spanish name for a rich stew, a kind of *cocido*, with an equally wide range of ingredients.

Peaches: it is hard to follow Castelvetro's logic when he quotes a proverb which says that one peels a fig for a friend but a peach for an enemy. Peeling a peach and dunking it in the remains of one's wine makes a pleasant after-dinner ritual, necessitating refills of the glass, for one's health's sake of course, and more peaches to finish off the wine . . .

Pepper, *Piper nigrum*, has been used since Roman times to give heat and pungency to food. Long pepper, *P. longum*, has a similar effect but is less aromatic and by Castelvetro's time was only used medicinally. Chillies, from the New World, were known to botanists and collectors of rare plants, but not used in the kitchen until later.

Pomegranates can be bought quite easily and are more fun to cook with than to eat as a dessert fruit. The tedious business of getting the juicy globules away from the tenaciously surrounding membranes, only to grapple with a mouthful of pips, is not rewarding. Far better to squeeze the juices out carefully by hand and make yourself a 'Stobart Special' (equal quantities of Dutch gin and pomegranate juice, chilled).

If you squeeze the pomegranates too vigorously the juice will become astringent with tannin from the membranes, so crush the fruit gently by hand and strain the juices through a sieve. The simplest way of using pomegranate juice is to dribble a brilliant pool of red juice on to a dish as you serve it. A more subtle use is in cooked sauces, either the Middle Eastern *fesenjan*, duck, pheasant or chicken with a pomegranate and walnut sauce, or simply stirred into the juices from a roast, which you could thicken with ground almonds or walnuts and a knob of butter. But select your pomegranate with care, for those sold in English green-grocers are sweet and watery compared with the richer, sharper flavour of pomegranates in Italy or the Middle East.

The bright pink seeds were used to decorate the medieval *biancoman-giare*, a sludge-like mixture of pounded chicken breasts, ground almonds, ground rice or breadcrumbs simmered together in clear chicken stock and perfumed with cinnamon and rosewater, which must have needed all the help it could get, visually speaking. Pomegranate seeds enliven any pale sauce that also needs their fruity astringency, and they add an unexpected piquancy to a mixed green salad.

Castelvetro thought a lot of the health-giving properties of pomegranate juice. Pomegranate wine was one of the things on his list of treasures to send from Italy to his friends in Sweden.

Pumpkins, gourds and squashes, which are members of the Cucurbita family, came from the New World; the ones Castelvetro describes would have been from the Lagenaria family, which were introduced into Europe in Roman times. They all need thoughtful cooking, to avoid wateriness, and can be good fried or simmered in a delicate-flavoured stock. My local Turkish bakery makes little pumpkin pasties with a filling of pumpkin purée, buttery semolina and raisins, flavoured with cinnamon and allspice.

Purslane has small, rounded, fleshy leaves, which are crisp and slightly bitter. It can be bought in Cypriot and Turkish stores in London and makes a pleasant addition to a salad, or can be eaten on its own. I am always told to put chopped onion with it, just as Castelvetro says.

Quinces: some of the varieties described by Castelvetro can be bought in London today, imported from Turkey, Cyprus and Australia. They are larger and less aromatic than English quinces, but pleasant stuffed with meat and spices, or added to Moroccan *tagines*, or cooked in a casserole with pheasants, butter and whisky or quince-flavoured vodka. English quinces, however, have the best fragrance and are ideal for making liqueurs, desserts and jellies.

Rhubarb, powdered, was the active ingredient in Castelvetro's remedy for chronic constipation, not the raisins to which he attributed its success. The raisins, softened in dry Malmsey wine, must have mitigated the horrible taste of the rhubarb however.

Salads: Castelvetro had suffered on his travels from badly prepared salads and his Sacred Law of Salads is precisely expressed: toss the clean, carefully dried leaves with salt and then with plenty of oil, and finally stir in a little vinegar.

Sorb-apples grow wild all over Italy. They are hard and sour but become aromatic and edible when bletted, ripened to the point of rottenness. Sorbs are good in jellies made from other hedgerow fruit such as sloes or rosehips.

Stitch, a violent pain in the chest, was probably pleurisy.

Stock is called for in many of Castelvetro's vegetable dishes; I prefer to translate it as 'broth', which is what it was, the rich, aromatic cooking liquid from simmering pots of meat or chicken, a prerequisite for the tasty vegetable stews he likes so much. It is not a good idea to use commercial stock cubes in any of Castelvetro's recipes. It is better to put aside some of the juices from a roast or a rich stew, or do without, getting the required richness from butter or cheese.

Sugar was still an expensive luxury in Castelvetro's time. It was used more as a seasoning than a sweetener, except by the very rich. Many recipes which shock us with the use of sugar in savoury meat dishes are not in fact sweet – the sugar accentuates the other flavours and makes a wonderful contrast to the sharpness of a sour juice or the aromas of spices. It was preferred to honey because it could be powdered and sprinkled on food; sometimes too, the flavour of honey was thought to be too obtrusive.

Sugolo was made by boiling must, unfermented grape juice, with flour into a thick paste. It kept well and made a pleasant, chewy sort of paste. I have not found this in Italy today, but a version of *sugolo* can be bought in Cypriot and Turkish shops in London – *sucuk*, sausage-shaped strips made of grape juice boiled up with flour, honey and rosewater, and stuffed with almonds.

Swine cress, *Coronopus squamatus*, is the most likely translation of *erba stella*, but this name was also given, confusingly, to lady's mantle, *Saxifraga rotundifolia* and *Plantago coronopus*.

Tortelli: the word is a diminutive of *torta*, pie or tart or pasty. Castelvetro's *tortelli* were made with thin pasta dough or pastry and fried in oil. Today we have recipes for *tortellini* made with pasta dough and stuffed with delicate mixtures of *ricotta* and herbs, or spinach or pumpkin purée, and cooked in water, which are very different from Castelvetro's crisp little pastries. There are many regional variations, with different names.

Truffles were a luxury in Castelvetro's time, but he ate them cooked on their own like mushrooms, so they cannot have been as expensive as they are now, when most of us can only hope for a scraping to perfume other dishes.

Verjuice, see **Agresto.**

Walnuts are indeed good eaten when young, before they are dried, but they must be really fresh or the bitter skins will have tainted the moist white flesh of the nuts.

Agliata (see separate entry) is a sauce made from walnuts. Walnut oil was used on furniture as teak oil is today.

Water chestnuts are the nut-like fruit of a water plant, *Trapa natans*, which are eaten boiled or roasted. They are not the same as Chinese water chestnuts, which are tubers (*Eleocharis tuberosa*).

Watermelon seeds are eaten, roasted and salted, in most Middle Eastern countries, as are the seeds of melons and pumpkins. There is an art in cracking the roasted shells open and extracting the tiny seed with tongue and teeth, while watching television or reading in bed or waiting for the bus. The vitamin content of the nuts is high, but so is the salt.

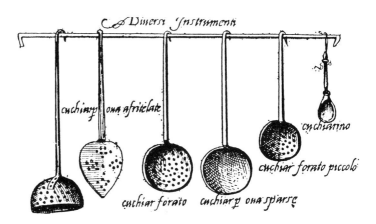

Bibliography

Arber, Agnes. *Herbals, Their Origin and Evolution*, Cambridge, 1938.

Blunt, Wilfrid and Raphael, Sandra. *The Illustrated Herbal*, London, 1979.

Brunetti, Gino. *Cucina mantovana di principi e di popolo*, Mantua, 1963.

Butler, K. T. 'An Italian's message to England in 1614: "Eat more fruit and vegetables"', *Italian Studies*, II, 1938, pp. 1–8.

Butler, K. T. 'Giacomo Castelvetro, 1546–1616', *Italian Studies*, V, 1950, pp. 1–18.

Carnacina, Luigi and Veronelli, Luigi. *La cucina rustica regionale*, Milan, 1966.

Carnporesi, Piero. *Bread of Dreams*, London, 1989.

Codacci, Leo. *Civiltà della tavola contadina*, Florence, 1981.

Coltro, Dino. *La cucina tradizionale veneta*, Rome, 1983.

Corato, Ricardo Di. *838 frutti e verdure d'Italia*, Milan, 1979.

Corato, Ricardo Di. *2214 vini d'Italia*, Milan, 1975.

Corato, Ricardo Di. *928 condimenti d'Italia*, Milan, 1978.

Cretì, Giorgio. *Erbe e malerbe in cucina*, Milan, 1987.

David, Elizabeth. *Italian Food*, new edn, London, 1987.

Dimsey, Sheila E. 'Giacopo Castelvetro', *Modern Language Review*, 23, 1928, pp. 424–31.

Evelyn, John. *Acetaria, a Discourse of Sallets*, London, 1699.

Faccioli, Emilio. *Arte della cucina*, Milan, 1966.

Faccioli, Emilio. *L'eccellenza e il trionfo del porco*, Emilia Romagna, 1982.

Faccioli, Emilio, ed. *Giacomo Castelvetro, Brieve racconto di tutte le radici di tutte l'erbe e di tutti i frutti che crudi o cotti in Italia si mangiano*, Mantua, 1988.

Firpo, Luigi. *Gastronomia del rinascimento*, Turin, 1973–4.

Gray, Patience. *Honey from a Weed*, London, 1986.

Grieve, M. *A Modern Herbal*, ed. and introduced by Mrs C. F. Leyel, London, 1931; Penguin Books, 1976.

Grigson, Jane. *Jane Grigson's Vegetable Book*, London, 1978; Penguin Books, 1980.

Grigson, Jane. *Jane Grigson's Fruit Book*, London, 1982; Penguin Books, 1983.

Hess, Karen. *Martha Washington's Booke of Cookery*, New York, 1981.

Lee, Maurice, Jr, ed. *Dudley Carleton to John Chamberlain 1603–1624: Jacobean Letters*, New Brunswick, 1972.

Libro contenente la maniera di cucinare e vari segreti e rimedi per malatie et altro, edited by Giulio Bizzarri and Eleonora Bronzoni, Ancona, 1986.

Maffioli, Giuseppe. *La cucina padovana*, Padua, 1981.

Meloni, Silvia. 'Giovanna Garzoni, miniatora medicea', *FMR*, 15, luglio/agosto 1983.

Morgan, Florence Humphreys. 'A Biography of Lucy Countess of Bedford, the Last Great Literary Patroness', unpublished PhD thesis, University of Southern California, January 1956.

Palmer, Richard. 'La botanica medica nell'Italia del nord durante il rinascimento', *Di sana pianta: erbari e taccuini di sanità, le radici storiche della nuova farmacologia*, Modena, 1988.

Pisanelli, Baldassare. *Trattato della natura de' cibi et del bere*, Venice, 1611.

Platina, Bartolomeo. *Il piacere onesto e la buona salute*, ed. Emilio Faccioli, Turin, 1985.

Rhodes, Denis E. 'The Italian banquet, 1598, and its origins', *Italian Studies*, vol. 27, 1972, pp. 60–63.

Roden, Claudia. *The Food of Italy*, Chatto & Windus, 1989.

Rosenberg, Eleanor. 'Giacopo Castelvetro, Italian publisher in Elizabethan London and his patrons', *Huntingdon Library Quarterly*, 2, Feb. 1943, pp. 119–48.

Rosengarten, Frederic, Jr. *The Book of Spices*, New York, 1973.

Sandonnini, T. *Ludovico Castelvetro e la sua famiglia*, Bologna, 1882.

Sandri, Amedeo, and Falloppi, Maurizio. *La cucina vicentina*, Padua, 1980.

Spike, John T. *Italian Still Life Paintings from Three Centuries*, New York, 1983.

Spurling, Hilary. *Elinor Fettiplace's Receipt Book, Elizabethan Country House Cooking*, London, Viking, 1986; Penguin Books, 1987.

Stobart, Tom. *The Cook's Encyclopaedia*, London, 1980.

Stobart, Tom. *Herbs, Spices and Flavourings*, London, 1970; Penguin Books, 1977.

Strong, Roy. *The Renaissance Garden in England*, London, 1979.

Thick, Malcolm. In Thirsk, Joan, ed., *The Agrarian History of England and Wales*, V, 2, Cambridge, 1985, pp. 503–32.

Zuliani, Mariu Salvatori de. *A tola coi nostri veci, la cucina veneziana*, Milan, 1978.

Manuscript sources

National Library of Scotland, Edinburgh

Adv. MS. 23–1–6. Ragionamento di Carlo V, Imperatore, tenuto al Re Philippo suo figliuolo. 1592

Trinity College, Cambridge

Castelvetro spent the last years of his life in the household of Sir Adam Newton. The Castelvetro books and papers came into the possession of Sir Adam's son, Henry, who took the name Puckering when he inherited the estate and title of Sir John Puckering, the Lord Keeper. The Puckering library was left to Trinity College, Cambridge, in the late seventeenth century, and embedded in it are many manuscripts in Castelvetro's hand. The ones which are relevant to this study are listed below:

Three versions of *Brieve racconto di tutte le radici, di tutte l'erbe e di tutti i frutti, che crudi o cotti in Italia si mangiano* in Castelvetro's handwriting:

R.14.19. dated 14 June 1614.

R.3.44. dated 28 June 1614, dedicated to 'Il signore Girolamo Biedo, Il Senatore'. This copy contains many reworkings and alterations.

R.3.44a. dated 28 September 1614.

R.10.6. Italian conversations. A rough draft of a conversation manual prepared by Castelvetro for some of the Cambridge students to whom he taught Italian in 1613.

R.10.7. A fair copy of a version of this manual, not in Castelvetro's hand.

R.4.24. 'Pezzi d'historia …' a translation by Castelvetro of political writings by Antonio Perez, in Castelvetro's handwriting. 'Il vulgarizzamento di questo libro fu per ispetial favore di Dio, compiuto da Giacopo Castelvetri modonese a xiii di Febraio MDCVII et incomminciato ma diverse fiate tralasciate per vari impedimenti sopravenutigli a xxiv di novembre del MDCV in

Vinegia. Ne prima l'ha riscritto come qui hora si vede, al netto, se non hoggi, ch'e Lunedi, terzo giorno del MDCXI nella stessa citta, del quale favore egli si rende all'eterno Iddio, tutte le gratie maggiori che sa, et piu.'

At least fifteen other volumes of political writings, either in Castelvetro's hand, or with annotations by him, are among the Puckering papers. They seem to have been written, or copied, by Castelvetro during his last years in Venice or his exile in England.

R.4.36. 'Italian tracts' contains 'Eccellente trattato della mercalantie de Preti …' Charlton, viii Agosto 1614, finished xi Ottobre 1614; 'Insegnamento di quelle particelle della vulgar lengua che turbano piu gli stranieri che ad'appararla si danno' is written in a copyist's hand, with corrections and alterations by Castelvetro.

The same volume contains the story of Giulietta, written in Castelvetro's rough script, an innocent young girl whose rendezvous with her lover in the local cemetery ended in tragedy.

R.14.36. Alchemical tract: 'Libro per certo d'oro, come della contenenza delle sue principali materie, posta nella facciata seguente chi leggera ben tosto vedra. In Venetia rescritto d'originale antico, l'anno di salute MDCIV.' Written in a copyist's hand, with titles and introduction by Castelvetro. Some 'segreti medicinali'.

R.14.47. 'I rari e non mai stampati secreti medicinali dell'eccellente fisico et filosofo Sr. Tadeo Duni medico principale di Zurico vivente, e che passa ottanta sette anni. Havuti del MDCXII in Zurico.'

Add. 9282. *Brieve racconto di tutte le radici, di tutte l'herbe et di tutti i frutti, che crudi o cotti in Italia si mangiano.*   *British Library, London*

Sloane 912. *Brieve racconto di tutte le radici, di tutte l'herbe e di tutti i frutti, che crudi o cotti in Italia si mangiano.*

Harley 3344. *Album amicorum*, inscribed on the flyleaf in the hand of the Cambridge antiquary, Thomas Baker: 'Jacobus Castelvetri, his Album, who lived and probably died in the house of Sir Adam Newton …'

British Museum,
Natural History

M. S. Banks 91. *Brieve racconto di tutte le radici, di tutte l'herbe e di tutti i frutti, che crudi o cotti in Italia si mangiano.* This is the copy dedicated to Lucy, Countess of Bedford. Castelvetro wrote out the dedication himself, the rest of the MS is written in an elegant French hand by a professional scribe.

Acknowledgements

I have selected illustrations which are for the most part contemporary with Castelvetro, and reflect the interest shown in Italy and Europe in the fruit and vegetables he described, from early herbals, botanical illustrations, still-life paintings and kitchen and market scenes. I am indebted to Dr A. C. Zeven and Dr W. A. Brandenburg of the Agriculture University at Wageningen, Marijke Kinkelder of the Rijksbureau Kunsthistorische Documentatie, The Hague, Françoise Berserik, and Ancilla Antonini of Index, for help in obtaining pictures.

My thanks are also due to the Master and Fellows of Trinity College, Cambridge, for permission to study the Castelvetro material in the Wren Library, and for the use of their MSS of the *Brieve racconto* in this translation. The Botanical Library of the British Museum, Natural History, made available the MS dedicated to the Countess of Bedford, on which this translation is based, and provided generous help with the illustrations.

I am also grateful to the following for their generous help and encouragement: Luigi and Anna Balsamo, Nicolas Barker, Treld Bicknell, Paul Breman, Alan Davidson, Giorgio Fini, Philip Gaskell, Patience Gray, Mary Greco and Diana Thomas, Jane Grigson, the Lancellotti restaurant, Sarah Martin, David McKitterick, Dr D. N. Pegler, Denis Rhodes, Professor W. T. Stearn, John Tyldesley, and the staff of the Botanic Library, British Museum, Natural History. I am particularly grateful to my editor, Caroline Davidson, for all her help with this project, and to James Mosley, who first drew my attention to the Castelvetro manuscripts and has been a constant support throughout.

The publisher and author are grateful to the following institutions for the loan of transparencies and their permission to reproduce them:

Biblioteca Mediceo Laurenziana, Florence, 51; Bibliothèque Nationale, Paris, 8, 48, 73, 104; Bridgeman Art Library, London, 70, 80–81, 115, 121, 122–3, 126, 136, 140–41, 144, 148–9; British Library, London, 16, 36, 37, 64, 75; British Museum, Natural History, Botanical Library, 42, 58, 60, 79, 91, 102, 118, 134; British Museum, Prints and Drawings, 6, 20, 33, 34, 35, 39, 43, 55, 63, 85, 116; Centraal

A Note on the Typeface

Galliard was drawn by Matthew Carter for Linotype in 1978. It is based on roman and italic types made by Robert Granjon (1513–c. 1589), a French punchcutter who made types for the printer Christophe Plantin in Antwerp and ended his life in Rome, making Arabic and other oriental types for the missionary press of Cardinal Ferdinando de' Medici. Granjon was a member of the younger generation of punchcutters who developed the classic style established by Claude Garamond, with whose roman types his lively italics were generally mated. Granjon's types are distinguished from those of his contemporaries by their spirit and vigour.

The set of type ornaments used in this book is found in an Arabic work bearing Granjon's name printed in Rome in 1584. It is used in the books of other Roman printers of the sixteenth and seventeenth centuries and was later cast in the Netherlands and England, where it was among the stock of the University Press at Oxford. It can probably be attributed to Granjon himself.

Index

(*Italic* numerals indicate the main reference)

Index